UNIVERSITY ASSOCIATES
Publishers and Consultants

SERIES IN HUMAN RELATIONS TRAINING

Reference Guide
to Handbooks
and Annuals

(Revised)

Volumes I-VIII and
'72-'81 Annuals

J. William Pfeiffer, Ph.D.
La Jolla, California

John E. Jones, Ph.D.
San Diego, California

UNIVERSITY ASSOCIATES
Publishers and Consultants
8517 Production Avenue
P.O. Box 26240
San Diego, California 92126

Copyright © 1981 by International Authors, B.V.

ISBN: 0-88390-069-6

Library of Congress Catalog Card Number 75-14661

The materials that appear in this book may be freely reproduced for educational/ training activities. There is no requirement to obtain special permission for such uses. We do, however, ask that the following statement appear on all reproductions:

> Reproduced from
> *Reference Guide to Handbooks and Annuals*
> (Revised)
> J. William Pfeiffer and John E. Jones
> San Diego, CA: UNIVERSITY ASSOCIATES, Inc., 1981

This permission statement is limited to reproduction of materials for educational/ training events. *Systematic or large-scale reproduction or distribution—or inclusion of items in publications for sale—may be done only with prior written permission.*

Printed in the United States of America

PREFACE

The eighteen books whose contents are classified in this edition of the *Reference Guide* contain a large number of useful materials—structured experiences, instruments, lecturettes, theory and practice papers, annotated bibliographies, and resources. Access to these tools, techniques, and ideas is made difficult by the serial nature of their publication. Occasionally even we, the editors, find it frustrating not to be able to locate a particular structured experience or paper in a hurry.

Earlier versions of the *Reference Guide* were received so enthusiastically by users of the Pfeiffer and Jones Series in Human Relations Training that we decided to improve its usefulness and expand its coverage. This edition includes classifications of *all* the contents of the eight volumes of *A Handbook of Structured Experiences for Human Relations Training* and the ten volumes of *The Annual Handbook for Group Facilitators*. The structured experiences have been classified differently this year, in a way that we think will enhance the user's ability to discriminate among and select from them. There are six major categories and forty-five subcategories. Readers of our older editions will recognize that this new classification system is more specific as to content and intent.

In addition to categorizing contents, we have drawn together much of the material that we have written about the rapidly expanding developments in the human relations field. In the introductions to the sections of the *Annuals* we have treated a number of topics related to the use of structured experiences, instruments, and lecturettes. We have also commented on the shape and progress of theory and research. These useful background materials have been collected and integrated into this revised *Reference Guide*.

We intend to update this publication periodically to incorporate new material that we have issued. Suggestions for improvement in format and content are welcomed.

We are also interested in continuing to receive manuscripts for possible inclusion in the Pfeiffer and Jones Series in Human Relations Training. Users may submit structured experiences, instruments, lecturettes, theory and practice papers, and comments on resources available to the practicing group facilitator and organization development consultant. We have developed an informational pamphlet to guide contributors in preparing manuscripts for our review; copies are available on request.

The original idea for a reference guide was developed by René Robitaille, who was enrolled in the first year of our Laboratory Education Intern Program. We are grateful for his contribution. In addition, we want to acknowledge Arlette Ballew, senior staff editor, who has coordinated several editions of the *Reference Guide*.

The *Handbooks* and the *Annuals* now appear in several foreign languages. We are very pleased to be instrumental in making these materials widely available to persons interested in improving the private and working lives of others. We also are gratified that the number of people who use our materials continues to increase every year. Our publishing aim is to share the useful and valuable information that we collect in the human relations training field. It is in this spirit that the *Reference Guide to Handbooks and Annuals* is prepared.

J. William Pfeiffer
La Jolla, California

John E. Jones
San Diego, California

December, 1980

TABLE OF CONTENTS

Instrumentation

Lecturettes

Theory and Practice

INTRODUCTION

The *Reference Guide to Handbooks and Annuals* is intended for use by group facilitators, organization development (OD) consultants, students, and others interested in applied behavioral science. Because the book contains discussions of many facets of experience-based learning, it can be used as an ancillary text as well as a reference source.

Classifications of each of the types of material included in *A Handbook of Structured Experiences for Human Relations Training* and *The Annual Handbook for Group Facilitators* are preceded by introductory statements that provide background or related information. These materials have been taken from the introductions to the five sections of the *Annuals*. We have also included in its entirety our paper on design from the 1973 *Annual*.

In each section—structured experiences, instruments, lecturettes, theory and practice papers, and resources—the titles are first organized into appropriate categories according to subject area and then, within each category, listed in order of their publication date. Following these five sections are name and title indexes.

This guide can be used in several ways. It can be studied for its collected information on the technology of human relations training. Facilitators can use it for design ideas for laboratories, workshops, conferences, meetings, seminars, institutes, and OD or HRD interventions. A particular piece published in the eighteen-book *Handbook* and *Annual* series can be located either by title or by author. Materials related to each other in subject matter, such as structured experiences and instruments in OD, can be cross-referenced.

CLASSIFICATION OF DESIGN COMPONENTS

The following chart[1] illustrates the relationship between learner involvement and the locus of meaning in human relations training. With *experiential* approaches—those that primarily stress active participant involvement vs. passive receptivity—the learning is presumably internalized more effectively.

Reading along the bottom of the chart, we see a classification of human relations training design components, ordered according to the extent to which they incorporate learner involvement. The least involving intervention is reading, in which the learner is in a *reactive* mode, passively receiving and vicariously experiencing. The most involving intervention is the intensive growth group, in which the learner is encouraged to be *proactive*, to take responsibility for his own learning. In between these two extremes are activities that range from lectures to structured experiences.

---

[1]Based in part on Hall, J., *The Awareness Model: A Rationale of learning and its application to individual and organizational practices*, Conroe, TX: Teleometrics, 1971; and Tannenbaum, R., & Schmidt, W.H., "How to Choose a Leadership Pattern," *Harvard Business Review*, May-June 1973, pp. 162-164, 166-168.

THE TECHNOLOGY OF HUMAN RELATIONS TRAINING

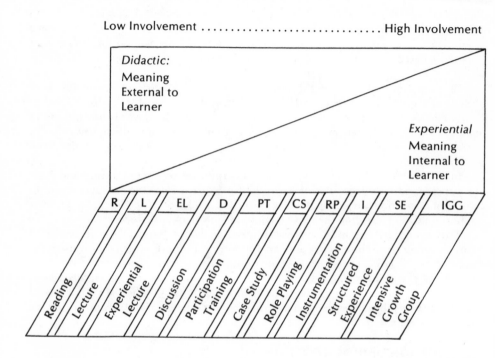

The experiential lecture is more involving than the traditional lecture because it incorporates activities on the part of the "audience." Interspersed among the sections of content are brief interactions among participants. These interruptions are designed either to personalize the points of the lecture and/or to generate readiness for the next topic.

Discussion is a time-honored teaching intervention that has been extended and refined in participation training, particularly by adult educators at Indiana University. The case-study method, popular in business education, is closely related to role playing, in which a "case" is acted out in a semistructured format.

In instrumentation, which involves learners in self-assessment, the didactic component comes from the theory underlying the items of the scale. Structured experiences stress high participation and "processing" of data generated during interactive activities.

Intensive growth groups exist in many forms, such as counseling, T-groups, encounter, and therapy. They are characterized by high learner involvement and interaction. The data for learning come from the life experiences and here-and-now reactions of the group members. Participants are expected to integrate their learning into new self-concepts on their own terms.

The involvement continuum in the chart can be seen in the same relationship to other dimensions, such as risk, self-disclosure, and interaction. Each design component is useful for a different purpose, and there are training situations in which each would be appropriate.

Facilitators are continually faced with the task of planning activities to meet the learning needs of participants. The design problem can be represented graphically as follows:

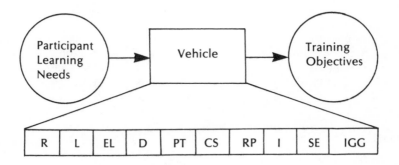

The choice of an effective intervention is made after an assessment of the learning needs of participants and a statement of training objectives. The maturity of the group, the skill and experience of the facilitator, and the environment in which the training takes place determine which approach is used.

AN EXPERIENTIAL MODEL

Experiential learning occurs when a person engages in some activity, looks back at the activity critically, abstracts some useful insight from the analysis, and puts the result to work. Of course, this process is experienced spontaneously in everyone's ordinary living. We call it an *inductive* process: proceeding from observation rather than from a priori "truth" (as in the *deductive* process). Learning can be defined as a relatively stable change in behavior, and that is the usual purpose of training. A *structured* experience provides a framework in which the inductive process can be facilitated. The steps follow those of a theoretical cycle.

The Experiential Learning Cycle

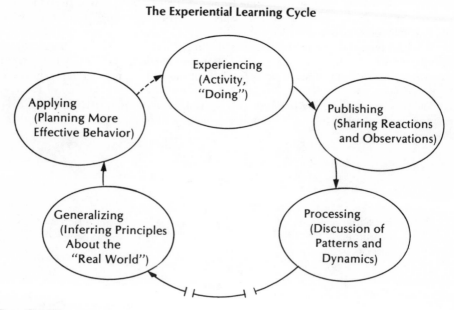

Experiencing

The initial stage is the data-generating part of the structured experience. It is the step that is often associated with "games," or fun. Obviously, if the process stops after this stage, all learning is left to chance, and the facilitator has not completed the task. Almost any activity that involves either self-assessment or interpersonal interaction can be used as the "doing" part of experiential learning. The following are common individual and group activities:

- making products
- creating art objects
- writing skits
- role playing
- transactions
- problem solving
- feedback
- self-disclosure
- fantasy
- choosing
- nonverbal communication
- writing
- analysis of case material
- bargaining

- planning
- competing
- confronting

These activities can be carried out by individuals, dyads, triads, small groups, group-on-group arrangements, or large groups. Of course, the learning objectives would dictate both the activity and the appropriate groupings.

It is important to note that the objectives of structured experiences are necessarily general and are stated in terms such as "to explore . . . ," "to examine . . . ," "to study . . . ," "to identify . . . ," etc. Inductive learning means learning through discovery, and the exact things to be learned cannot be specified beforehand. All that is wanted in this stage of the learning cycle is to develop a common data base for the discussion that follows. This means that whatever happens in the activity, whether expected or not, becomes the basis for critical analysis; participants may learn serendipitously.

Sometimes facilitators spend an inordinate amount of energy planning the activity but leave the examination of it unplanned. As a consequence, learning may not be facilitated. It is axiomatic that the next four steps of the experiential learning cycle are even more important than the experiencing phase. Accordingly, the facilitator needs to be careful that the activity does not generate excess data or create an atmosphere that makes discussion of the results difficult. There can be a lot of excitement and "fun" as well as conflict in human interaction, but these are not synonymous with learning; they provide the common references for group inquiry.

Publishing

The second stage of the cycle is roughly analogous to inputting data, in data-processing terms. People have experienced an activity, and now they are presumably ready to share what they saw and/or how they felt during the event. The intent here is to make available to the group the experience of each individual. This step involves finding out what happened within individuals, at both cognitive and affective levels, while the activity was progressing. A number of methods help to facilitate the publishing, or declaring, of the reactions and observations of individual participants:

- Recording data during the experiencing stage (putting data "in the can" for later discussion): ratings of such things as productivity, satisfaction, confidence, communication, etc.; adjectives capturing feelings at various points.
- Whips: quick free-association go-arounds on various topics concerning the activity.
- Subgroup sharing: generating lists such as the double-entry one "What we saw/how we felt."
- Posting/roundrobin listing: total-group input recorded on newsprint.
- Ratings: developing ratings of relevant dimensions of the activity, tallying and averaging these measures.

- Go-around: systematic "interviewing" of individuals about their experience during the activity.
- Nominations: variation of "Guess Who?" technique, asking participants to nominate each other for roles they played during the experiencing stage.
- Interviewing pairs: asking each other "what" and "how" questions about the activity.

Publishing can be carried out through free discussion, but this requires that the facilitator be absolutely clear about the differences in the steps of the learning cycle and distinguish sharply among interventions in the discussion. Group members' energy is often focused on staying inside the activity, and they need to be nudged into separating themselves from it in order to learn. (See, for example, the discussion of "de-roling" role players, on page 191 of the 1979 *Annual.*) Structured techniques such as those listed above make the transition from stage one to stage two cleaner and easier. That, after all, is the job of the facilitator—to create clarity with ease.

Processing

This stage can be thought of as the fulcrum, or the pivotal step in experiential learning. It is the systematic examination of commonly shared experience by those persons involved. This is the "group dynamics" phase of the cycle, in which participants essentially reconstruct the patterns and interactions of the activity from the published individual reports. This "talking-through" part of the cycle is critical, and it cannot be either ignored or designed spontaneously if useful learning is to be developed. The facilitator needs to plan carefully how the processing will be carried out and focused toward the next stage, generalizing. Unprocessed data can be experienced as "unfinished business" by participants and can distract them from further learning. Selected techniques that can be used in the processing stage are listed below:

- Process observers: reports, panel discussions (observers are often unduly negative and need training in performing their functions).
- Thematic discussion: looking for recurring topics from the reports of individuals.
- Sentence completion: writing individual responses to such items as "The leadership was . . . ," "Participation in this activity led to . . . ."
- Questionnaires: writing individual responses to items developed for the particular structured-experience activity (for example, see "Motivation Feedback Opinionnaire" in the Structured Experiences section of the 1973 *Annual*).
- Data analysis: studying trends and correlations in ratings and adjectives elicited during the publishing stage.
- Key terms: posting a list of dimensions to guide the discussion.
- Interpersonal feedback: focusing attention on the effect of the role behaviors of significant members in the activity.

This step should be thoroughly worked through before going on to the next. Participants should be led to look at what happened in terms of dynamics but not in terms of "meaning." What occurred was real, of course, but it was also somewhat artificially contrived by the structure of the activity. It is important to keep in mind that a consciousness of the dynamics of the activity is critical for learning about human relations outside of the laboratory setting. Participants often anticipate the next step of the learning cycle and make premature generalization statements. The facilitator needs to make certain that the processing has been adequate before moving on.

Generalizing

An inferential leap has to be made at this point in the structured experience, from the reality inside the activity to the reality of everyday life outside the training session. The key question here is "So what?" Participants are led to focus their awareness on situations in their personal or work lives that are similar to those in the activity that they experienced. Their task is to abstract from the processing some principles that could be applied "outside." This step is what makes structured experiences practical, and if it is omitted or glossed over the learning is likely to be superficial. Here are some strategies for developing generalizations from the processing stage:

- Fantasy: guiding participants to imagine realistic situations "back home" and determining what they have learned in the discussion that might be applicable there.
- Truth with a little "t": writing statements from the processing discussion about what is "true" about the "real world."
- Individual analysis: writing "What I learned," "What I'm beginning to learn," "What I re-learned."
- Key terms: posting topics for potential generalizations, such as leadership, communication, feelings, etc.
- Sentence completion: writing completions to items such as "The effectiveness of shared leadership depends on . . . ."

It is useful in this stage for the group interaction to result in a series of products—generalizations that are presented not only orally but also visually. This strategy helps to facilitate vicarious learning among participants. The facilitator needs to remain nonevaluative about what is learned, drawing out the reactions of others to generalizations that appear incomplete, undivided, or controversial. Participants sometimes anticipate the final stage of the learning cycle also, and they need to be kept on the track of clarifying what was learned before discussing what changes are needed.

In the generalizing stage it is possible for the facilitator to bring in theoretical and research findings to augment the learning. This practice provides a framework for the learning that has been produced inductively and checks the reality orientation of the process. But the practice may encourage dependence on the facilitator as the source of defensible knowledge and may lessen commitment to the final stage of the cycle. The outside information is not "owned" by the participants—a common phenomenon of *deductive* processes.

Applying

The final stage of the experiential learning cycle is the purpose for which the whole structured experience is designed. The central question here is "Now what?" The facilitator helps participants apply generalizations to actual situations in which they are involved. Ignoring such discussion jeopardizes the probability that the learning will be useful. It is critical that attention be given to designing ways for individuals and/or groups to use the learning generated during the structured experience to plan more effective behavior. Several practices can be incorporated into this stage:

- Consulting dyads or triads: taking turns helping each other with back-home problem situations and applying generalizations.
- Goal-setting: writing applications according to such goal criteria as specificity, performance, involvement, realism, and observability (see the 1972 *Annual*, pp. 133-134).
- Contracting: making explicit promises to each other about applications.
- Subgrouping: in interest groups discussing specific generalizations in terms of what can be done more effectively.
- Practice session: role playing back-home situations to attempt changed behavior.

Individuals are more likely to implement their planned applications if they share them with others. Volunteers can be asked to report what they intend to do with what they learned, and this can encourage others to experiment with their behavior also.

It is important to note that on the diagram of the experiential learning cycle there is a dotted arrow from "applying" to "experiencing." This is meant to indicate that the actual application of the learning is a new experience for the participant, to be examined inductively also. What structured experiences "teach," then, is a way of using one's everyday experiences as data for learning about human relations. This is sometimes referred to as "relearning how to learn." Actually, there are other ways to learn. For example, skills are best learned through practice toward an ideal model, knowledge of results, and positive reinforcement. Also, structured experiences do not readily facilitate the development of large-scale perspective; lecture-discussion methods are probably superior for such a purpose. What experiential learning does accomplish, though, is a sense of ownership over what is learned. This is most easily achieved by making certain that each stage of the learning cycle is developed adequately.

REFERENCE

Jones, J.E., & Pfeiffer, J.W. (Eds.). *The 1973 annual handbook for group facilitators.* San Diego, CA: University Associates, 1973.

A GLOSSARY OF TERMS IN EXPERIENTIAL TRAINING

Human relations trainers are notorious for their use of jargon. Facilitators using an "applied-behavioral-science" approach often use technical terms interchangeably, adding to the confusion of participants. The following listing is intended to help clarify this situation.

Activity	Design for participation to create a common experience to be studied and discussed by participants.
Case Study	Group discussion and problem solving from material about an actual situation.
Critique	Group evaluation of the effective and ineffective aspects of a learning design.
Deductive	A learning method that begins with "truth" and proceeds to its logical conclusions.
Design Task	An assignment to create a plan for learning through interaction.
De-Roling	Helping participants in a role play to extricate themselves from their assigned roles and to resume their normal interactions.
Didactic	Adjective describing a teaching approach in which information is imparted from an expert.
Energizer	Activity designed to develop readiness for participation in learning events; usually involves physical movement and fun.
Exercise	Repetitive activity, usually designed as a part of training to develop skills.
Experience-Based	Synonymous with "Experiential."
Experiencing	Phase I of the "Experiential Learning Cycle"; a learning activity to be discussed by participants afterwards.
Experiential	Adjective describing an approach to learning in which participants in an activity learn through reflection on the activity itself.

Experiential Learning Cycle	Model of an inductive learning process consisting of five phases: Experiencing, Publishing, Processing, Generalizing, and Applying.
Experiment	A (structured) activity with unpredictable outcomes.
Facilitation	Helping participants learn from an activity; conducting experiential training.
Facilitator	Person who uses experiential methods to promote learning; literally, "one who makes things easy."
Feedback	Information about the effects of one's behavior.
Game	An activity that is engaged in for its own sake; usually connotes fun and competition or chance.
Ice Breaker	Activity to help participants to release anxiety at the beginning of a training event; usually fun, involving becoming acquainted with one another.
Inductive	A learning method that is based on the discovery of "truth" from the examination of experience.
Input	Exposition of information or theory; contribution to a discussion.
Instrument	Paper-and-pencil device used to inventory oneself or a system.
Instrumentation	The use of instruments in training or research.
Intensive Growth Group	Unstructured experience focused on the "here and now"; may be T-group, encounter, therapy, counseling, or marathon.
Item	Component of an instrument.
Likert Scale	Attitude-measurement scale developed by Rensis Likert; usually "strongly agree, agree, undecided, disagree, strongly disagree."

Model | (1) Theoretical explanation of a complex set of phenomena; (2) ideal behavior type.

Modeling | (1) Demonstrating effective behavior; (2) developing a theoretical explanation of a process.

Norms | (1) Expected behaviors; (2) statistical summary of responses to an instrument.

Package | Self-contained training design that is completely developed, with little or no flexibility.

Parameter | Boundary, limit; what the facilitator has to work with in creating a learning design.

Participation Training | Group discussion that includes learning how to be a more effective group member.

Processing | Group discussion of the results of a learning activity; Phase III of the Experiential Learning Cycle.

Publishing | Sharing reactions and observations; talking about one's experience during a learning activity; Phase II of the Experiential Learning Cycle.

Questionnaire | An instrument that does not have correct answers; used in surveys.

Reinforcement | Anything that raises the probability that a response will be repeated.

Response Format | Scale or method used by participants in reacting to the items of an instrument.

Role Playing | Design for learning in which participants act out a situation through assigned parts that they play spontaneously.

Self-Assessment | Looking inward at oneself, usually through a learning activity.

Self-Disclosure | Communicating about oneself to others; usually connotes letting others know about one's private self.

Set — Psychological condition prior to an activity; attitudinal predisposition; expectations.

Simulation — Interactive learning package designed to re-create or mirror a larger, more complex situation in order to sponsor learning.

Skill Building — Developing effective behavior through practice toward an ideal type, with both knowledge of results (feedback) and reinforcement.

Structured Experience — Design for inductive learning through the implementation of the Experiential Learning Cycle; focuses on particular learning goals.

Test — Instrument with "correct" answers.

Win-Lose — Adjective describing a competitive situation in which there must be a loser in order for there to be a winner.

Although these terms are not technically precise, we have found it useful to insist on making sharp distinctions between them for the sake of clarity and ease of comprehension. Undoubtedly many persons would argue for even more specific and exclusive definitions. We invented the term "structured experience," for example, to emphasize the two aspects of that intervention: the existence of some boundaries and the process of learning through doing.

DESIGN CONSIDERATIONS IN LABORATORY EDUCATION*

J. William Pfeiffer and John E. Jones
(Originally published in *The 1973 Annual Handbook for Group Facilitators*)

One of the most complex activities in which the group facilitator/human relations consultant is engaged is designing learning experiences for client systems. The purpose of this paper is to discuss some of the determinants of effectiveness in laboratory-education design in general and to explore the major elements that the facilitator needs to consider in designing laboratories based on experiential learning.

Whether one is planning a course in human relations, a weekend personal growth laboratory, or a management-development seminar, there are common concerns and questions that need to be considered in order for an optimum design to emerge. We will begin by cataloging the major parameters that need to be specified before designs can be built, the skills involved in designing laboratory-education events, components of the laboratory itself, and considerations that must be taken into account in meeting the unique needs of the client system. The primary emphasis is on integrating these general design considerations into an organic sequence of learning activities that are central to personal growth and skill-development laboratories. In addition, we have included suggestions concerning professional development in the area of design.

MAJOR DESIGN PARAMETERS

Before the design itself can be considered, several questions must be answered concerning the specific learning experience being planned. The purpose of this section is to provide an explicit check list of these concerns which the facilitator may use in testing his own readiness to begin the design process. He is ready to design when he has data about the following:

1. the contract
2. the length and timing of the event
3. the location and physical facilities
4. the familiarity of participants with each other
5. the training experience of the participants

---

*Laboratory education has been operationally defined by the International Association of Applied Social Scientists as events that include T-groups (semistructured) and D-groups (structured). This definitition *excludes* personal growth groups ("structureless"), which the organization defines in terms of psychotherapy—groups that have an emergent design rather than a previously planned design. However, the authors have some concern that the term "T-group" has come to incorporate a variety of meanings to professionals and to lay people, including some negative connotations; therefore, we prefer to use the term "personal growth" to denote semistructured dimensions that IAASS defines as T-group experiences.

6. the availability of qualified staff
7. the number of participants
8. access to materials and other aids
9. the opportunity for follow-through.

Contract. Although the previous list is not rank-ordered in terms of urgency, the first item is perhaps the most important. It is critical that the facilitator have a clear sense of what the contract between himself and the client system is. This consideration relates to his skill in specifying goals. It is important that he be able to narrow the expectation gap between himself and the participants in the laboratory. It is also important that he recognize that the psychological contract and the legal contract may not be the same. The design is far more likely to have a chance to be effective if the participants come into the learning experience knowing what to expect, why they are there, and what they have contracted to experience. The facilitator may choose to negotiate such a contract explicitly with the client system (e.g., Egan's model contract, contained in the 1972 *Annual*) or the facilitator may choose simply to rely on a word-of-mouth or a brochure procedure to specify the learning goals of the event. In any case, it is important that the goals and the learning method of the event be specified beforehand in language that both the staff and the participants can understand.

Length and Timing of the Event. The length and timing of the laboratory are important in that the sequencing and timing of particular events are dependent in part on whether the laboratory takes place en masse or is spaced over several meetings. The laboratory that runs weekly for an hour or two presents a significantly different design problem than a weekend event. In a brief contact design such as one evening or one or two days, some learning modules would not be attempted because either there would not be enough trust developed in the time available or more data might be generated than could be adequately processed.

Location and Physical Facilities. The third parameter is important in that it is easier to develop what is called a "cultural-island" effect in a retreat setting than it is in the ordinary, everyday environment of the participants. It is more possible in a retreat situation to capitalize on the development of norms of meaningful openness, experimentation, and sensitivity in creating an environment in which people are genuinely resourceful to each other during the free time of the laboratory event. It is often noted that some of the most significant learning in human relations training takes place outside these formally planned sessions. The physical facilities are critical; ordinarily the facilitator wants to have movable furniture and privacy for the training event. Auditoriums are usually too inflexible, and sometimes very large open spaces are detrimental to the laboratory design. It is also important to anticipate whether the training event is likely to be interrupted by nonparticipants, telephone calls, and other annoyances.

Familiarity of Participants with Each Other. This parameter is important in laboratory design in terms of selecting learning experiences. It may not be necessary to include "ice-breaker" activities with a group of people who are familiar with each other.

What often happens is that some participants know one another, but there is an unequal acquaintanceship within the group. The design of the laboratory should take into account that there might be some natural subdivision owing to previous social acquaintance outside the laboratory itself. It may be desirable to use this information in forming groups, assigning staff to the particular groups, and selecting activities for the beginning and the end of the experience. One may capitalize on the relationships that participants bring to a laboratory experience by using acquaintanceship as a means of support for planning back-home application and for follow-through.

Training Experience of Participants. Whether participants have been in laboratory-education programs before is important because they may already have experienced some training activities in which the learning depends on the novelty of the experience to the participants. It may be that the clients will have been engaged in activities highly similar to those that are being planned, and it makes sense to know something of the background of the participants in regard to experiential approaches to education before the design is attempted. People who have been in laboratory experiences before may be formed into an advanced group, they may be spread out deliberately across several learning groups, or they may be asked to volunteer for demonstrations of here-and-now interaction.

Availability of Qualified Staff. The sixth parameter is the availability of qualified staff to work as facilitators in the training program. The design of the experience should take into account the capabilities of the staff members as well as their preparedness in attempting various learning goals. If the staff members are minimally qualified, it may be necessary to use a great deal of instrumentation and structure to make up for their lack of supervised experience. The intensity level of a laboratory may be modified and controlled somewhat depending on the expertise of the available staff. Where the credentials of the staff are somewhat suspect, it may be necessary to develop fairly strict controls on the amount of affect that is generated in the laboratory experience itself. Activities that might generate a great deal of feeling data might not be used in the design because, in general, they require a great deal more expertise on the part of the staff.

Number of Participants. It is important to be able to anticipate how many people are likely to be involved in the laboratory setting because some laboratory design components require a large number of people while others are designed to be used with very small groups. In general, we recommend that there be co-facilitators in every intensive small group and that there be a pair of facilitators for about every ten to twelve participants.

Access to Materials and Other Aids. Availability, budget, and convenience should be considered prior to planning a laboratory. Some materials, such as standardized measurement instruments, are expensive, and others require a great deal of preparation time for their assembly. Some teaching aids, such as videotape recorders, are difficult to carry from place to place. The facilitator needs to develop an inventory of materials that are available both on-site and within his own resources: flip charts, chalkboards, overhead projectors and other audiovisual aids, as well as work sheets, instruments, and handouts. It is often very useful to have duplicating equipment at the laboratory setting.

Opportunity for Follow-Through. A final consideration deals with the opportunity to follow through with the laboratory participants after the experience is formally ended. Although this parameter is listed last, it is by no means of least importance. When developing a design for a learning event it is important to know beforehand what is going to happen afterwards. Is it going to be feasible for participants to meet again to work through the problems of transfer of training? Are they going to have access to each other on a day-to-day basis? Is the staff of the laboratory going to be accessible to them afterwards? Is it possible to have follow-up sessions some weeks or months later to ensure transfer of training? Part of the application of laboratory learning to the participants' own work and social settings can be designed differently if there is an opportunity for some support and follow-through work after the laboratory is completed.

Prior to developing the design for a particular training event, the facilitator needs to explore what he has to work with in terms of time, space, staff, money, human resources, and materials. Once he has completed such an inventory he may conclude that the contracted goals of the learning experience are unattainable given the resources that are available to him, and he may want to renegotiate the contract or attempt to develop new resources for the event.

DESIGN SKILLS

Goal Setting. The ability to develop a learning design that is relevant and effective is dependent on a number of skills on the part of the small-group facilitator. The major set of skills relates to the ability to identify the learning goals of the training event very specifically. It cannot be stressed enough that laboratory education is goal oriented, and it is important for the facilitator to learn ways to be able to clarify his goals for a particular training event or a particular part of a training event so that they are motivators for the particular learning experience itself. A closely related set of skills involves helping participants clarify their own goals. It is important that human relations training activities be carried out in reference to highly specific goals that are related to the behavior of the participants. In designing a laboratory, then, one begins with establishing, in a very specific way, the goals of the experience.

Sensitivity to Participant Response. A second set of skills in designing laboratory-education events is sensitivity to participant response. The facilitator learns to anticipate how participants are likely to react to particular components of the laboratory design. In addition, he becomes adept at anticipating the cumulative effects of the design. He should be able to make some probability statements about the receptivity of participants to particular learning experiences at a particular point in the laboratory. Part of this sensitivity involves acquaintanceship with the client system. It is important that the facilitator be able to know how participants are likely to react to particular structured experiences and to particular foci within the laboratory. For example, if the laboratory is to begin with a nonverbal activity, how much tension is this likely to create in this particular client system at this particular point in its development? How are the same participants likely to react to a similar activity after they have been together in a retreat setting for two days? Sensitivity to the probable participant response is developed from experience with a variety of learning activities, with a variety of clients, and with a great deal of staff discussion of experiences in similar learning situations.

Sequencing. Sequencing constitutes a third set of skills in laboratory design. Learning events are not put together in a random way; it is important that the facilitator be able to see the impact of one particular training component on the one that immediately follows it. Sometimes the objective is to close things down; at other times the objective may be to open things up in order for the next training module to be more effective. One of the major purposes of this paper is to expand the group facilitator's awareness of sequencing considerations in laboratory training designs.

Collaborating with Other Facilitators. A fourth array of skills involves collaborating with other facilitators. In our experience it is more effective and efficient for one facilitator to accept responsibility for the initial design of the laboratory-education event and to work with other facilitators to edit the design to make it more relevant to the learning needs of the participants in light of the goals of the training event. It is expensive to bring together a group of facilitators to build a design from ground zero. It is true that when staff members create a design themselves, from the beginning, they are more likely to have a sense of investment, involvement, and psychological ownership in what is planned. They are likely to approach the implementation of the design with more vigor. It is also true, however, that human relations training staffs ordinarily do not have a great deal of time to prepare for a particular event. We find it useful to have an initial, tentative design that the staff will edit rather than build one from the beginning. One of the major problems in designing laboratories centers around this set of skills. Many group facilitators have their own favorite ways of doing things and sometimes are reluctant to collaborate in experimenting with other teaching procedures. It is sadly ironic that we often become locked into particular ways of working in human relations training and violate our own norms of experimentation and innovation.

Modifying Designs. A fifth set of skills involves modifying designs while the laboratory is in progress. There is no way that any group facilitator can anticipate all the responses of the participants and all the real-time concerns that become relevant in producing a plan of activities for fostering client learning. The facilitator needs to develop the ability to change the learning design while the laboratory is running. This involves taking data from the participants about their own needs at a particular stage of the laboratory's development and finding appropriate alternatives to what was planned prior to the laboratory. When the facilitator discovers that what was planned back in the staff meeting before the laboratory began no longer makes sense in terms of what is happening now, he needs to be able to redirect the learning experience without becoming threatened by his lack of anticipation of participant response.

Skill in designing laboratory events involves learning how to make one's goals highly explicit and specific, learning to anticipate how particular participants are likely to respond to the various learning activities, learning to put laboratory components together in meaningful ways, developing the ability to collaborate with other facilitators in producing designs noncompetitively, and developing the ability to redirect the learning experience while it is in progress.

LABORATORY COMPONENTS

Designing human relations laboratories or leadership-development laboratories involves putting together sequences of learning experiences in relation to the goals of the event. Four major components are ordinarily utilized. Some combination of intensive small groups, structured experiences, lecturettes, and instruments is employed to develop a community of learners who can collaborate in achieving the goals of the laboratory. The purpose of this section is to discuss each of these four integral components of laboratory design.

Intensive Small Groups. An almost endless variety of small groups have been developed within human-interaction laboratories. The most common is the T-group, or training group, which is described in an earlier paper on types of growth groups (Jones, 1972). Other small-group designs incorporated into such things as personal growth and leadership-development laboratories include the D-group, or developmental group (Blake & Mouton, 1962). This is a group that uses a variety of questionnaires, rating scales, and other instruments and learning devices in the place of a trained facilitator. Sometimes laboratories include a variety of temporary groups that are put together on a short-term basis for processing the data of a particular learning experience. These groups are sometimes called N-groups, or new groups, assembled for the purpose of providing the opportunity for risk taking, trying of new behavior, or testing of back-home application ideas. In addition, it is sometimes desirable to build leaderless activities into laboratory events.

The dominant feature of laboratory education is the use of intensive small groups; this becomes the basic building block in laboratory design. Ordinarily one wants to build as much heterogeneity as possible into small-group composition, with the stipulation that there be enough commonality among participants so that any given participant can identify with at least one other person in the group. It is important to establish some home base within the learning experience—a place in which participants can experience support and safety and where they can attempt to integrate what they are learning about themselves. The intensive small-group experience becomes such a base in a laboratory.

Structured Experiences. A wide array of activities is available to the group facilitator in planning a design (e.g., Pfeiffer & Jones, 1969 & 1974; 1970 & 1974; 1971 & 1974; 1973; 1975; 1977; 1979, 1981). Any given activity may be equally appropriate in a personal growth design or in a laboratory focusing on team development, but since the goals of the two events may be significantly different, the processing of the data generated by the structured experience is decidedly different. For example, in a structured experience that we have used from time to time in laboratories, the facilitator distributes materials and gives the group members the task of organizing themselves to construct a checkerboard. In a basic human relations laboratory, the behavioral and feeling data that are generated by such an event would probably be processed in a T-group meeting in which people would focus on their own emerging awareness and on their feelings and reactions to other people's behavior. They would be given feedback of a very personal nature about the effects of the process and the effects of each other's behavior. In a leadership-development laboratory, the same event might be processed in terms of leadership styles that emerged during the event, styles of influence, roles people played, and decision-making procedures. There might also be an attempt to process the data in terms of a theory of leadership. Structured experiences generate and focus data toward particular learnings, but the major skill in their use is in adapting them to the particular learning needs of the participants in a given laboratory and in assisting participants in processing and integrating data that are generated by their use.

Lecturettes. The infusion of cognitive material into the laboratory experience is accomplished in several ways. One may deliver brief lectures (lecturettes) in large group sessions, commonly called "community" sessions. One may comment very quickly within an intensive small-group session about the theoretical implications of a particular set of behavioral data, one may provide a reading book prior to the laboratory experience, or one may give handouts during the experience itself. The facilitator needs to develop a repertoire of brief lecturettes that he can use to highlight particular processes at any given time in the laboratory's development. The Lecturettes section of the *Annual* is intended to provide a resource for such brief theoretical inputs into laboratory design. In the laboratory itself, lecturettes may be used prior to particular learning experiences to provide a kind of cognitive map for the experience that is about to ensue, or they may be used to help focus the data from a particular structured experience or intensive group meeting. They provide a way of helping participants "make sense out of" the learning that they are experiencing and they help to heighten the probability that the participant will relearn how to learn from his everyday experiences by providing him with cognitive models for guiding his behavior.

These brief lectures are aided considerably by visual presentations. Sometimes the use of a flip chart can make a particular lecturette easier to follow, and the outline of the lecturette can be posted for participants to read throughout the experience. A lecturette on the criteria of effective feedback, for example, can result in a poster listing such criteria, and during the laboratory, participants can be guided in giving and receiving feedback by a set of considerations that become internalized through the experience. Sometimes the posting of such theory material serves as a means of guiding participants' behavior without using staff members to remind them of particular learnings.

Instruments. Nonclinical measurement devices can be highly useful in a laboratory-education design. They can serve to focus on particular behavioral science concepts and can provide a set of data by which participants can explore themselves intra- and interpersonally, study group composition, and discover new behaviors that they might consider practicing within the relative safety of the laboratory milieu. The Instrumentation section of the *Annual* is designed to provide easy access to instruments that might be incorporated into laboratory designs. Our usual style is to introduce an instrument by encouraging participants to be very open in responding to the items, to ask participants to complete the scale, to lecture on the rationale underlying the instrument, to illustrate the interpretation of the scoring by using our own scores as examples, and to have participants practice interpreting each other's scores (usually in helping pairs). We often follow this by posting the data to build norms for the particular laboratory and then processing the data in intensive small-group meetings that tend to focus on the personal relevance of the data at a relatively higher support level than characterizes individual interpretation. Instruments are not substitutes for experiential approaches, but they can often serve as highly effective means of focusing learning around a theoretical model.

These four basic components—intensive small groups, structured experiences, lecturettes and instruments—can be varied almost infinitely to provide highly innovative, flexible designs to meet the learning needs of participants. In the next section we will deal with some major considerations within the laboratory itself to ensure that these components are utilized effectively.

GENERAL CONSIDERATIONS

Ten major considerations will be discussed in this section to guide the facilitator in the process of designing a laboratory. This list of major dimensions constitutes a compilation of *dos* and *don'ts* for the process of designing.

Investment and Involvement. In designing a human-interaction laboratory, it is important for the facilitator to plan not to have passive audiences at any time during the training event. Every participant needs to have something to do all the time during the formally planned sessions. If there is going to be a lecture, the facilitator will stress active listening. If he is using a structured experience, roles need to be assigned so that every person has something to do that contributes to his own learning within the context of that experience. The important thing is that from the very beginning each participant is led to accept the responsibility for his own learning within the laboratory context and that ample opportunity is given for him to act out his responsibility through participation.

Sequencing. Each activity within the laboratory should build from the previous sequence of activities and toward the next one. That is, every component of a laboratory design should fit into an ordered scheme that results in the attainment of the goals of the laboratory. The next section of this paper will contain a discussion of the unique sequencing concerns in personal growth and awareness- or skill-development designs. Balance should also be considered in the sequencing so that the participant does not get an overload of cognitive material. Even the meals should be strategically placed, and the effect of the interaction within the meals needs to be anticipated as one plans for the events that follow. Sometimes it is important in the sequence to have thematic material that runs throughout all the components of the laboratory design, thus allowing for the processing of a variety of events against the same theoretical model.

Content. It is highly desirable to use locally relevant content whenever possible. This is particularly true in leadership-development laboratories, in which the content of the activities needs to parallel closely the kinds of leadership concerns and problems that participants ordinarily face in their work. A number of data-generating techniques can be employed within the laboratory to ensure that the content of the learning design is relevant to the participants as they are experiencing it. There are several useful strategies.

Participants can be asked to make notes to themselves about particular feelings they are experiencing, thoughts they are thinking, persons to whom they are reacting, and so on. One useful technique is the "think-feel" card, on which participants are instructed to record their reactions at any particular point. On one side they are to write a sentence beginning with "I think," and on the other side they are to write a sentence beginning with "I feel." This process very often heightens participants' willingness to share these reactions with others.

A highly useful intervention in a group meeting or in other laboratory events is to form dyads and to ask the members of each pair to interview each other with regard to their reactions to a particular issue, event, or piece of behavioral datum at any given time. Often we ask people to use this as an exercise in active listening. Ordinarily the interviewer should not make notes but should frequently paraphrase what he hears to make certain that he is not translating in terms of his own reality rather than being sensitive to the phenomenological system of the person being interviewed.

A list of concerns can be generated rapidly on a flip chart or chalkboard. Such a list may include issues facing the group at any given moment, problems facing the group, controversial topics, persons, etc. Participants can be asked to rank-order the list according to some criterion such as urgency or influence. Often it is useful to ask participants first to perform a ranking independently to establish their own points of view and then to divide them into small groups, each to develop a consensus ranking of the material.

Questionnaires can be developed that include multiple-choice items, rating scales, open-ended questions, and so on. These can be used prior to or within the laboratory to generate data for participant learning. It is important that participants take the responsibility to process the data, and it may be desirable to post the statistical results so that the group can analyze itself.

It is sometimes helpful for a group to look back on its own history to analyze how it has used its time quantitatively. A list of topics that have constituted the group's agenda in past meetings can be generated, and the amount of energy that has been expended on any given item can be discussed. Sometimes a group discovers that an inordinate amount of energy has been expended on particular concerns and that it may be able to use its time more efficiently.

Videotaping is an excellent technique. It is extremely difficult to recapture much of the data generated in a learning event by depending on memory alone, and the advantages of videotape, with instant and repeated playback, are obvious. Nonverbal data can be highly focused by the use of this medium, and it is often very useful in teaching process awareness.

A group can look at its own development at any given moment through a problem-solving method called force-field analysis. A lecturette in the 1973 *Annual*, "Kurt Lewin's 'Force Field Analysis,' " describes this process.

Occasionally, teaching the distinction between content and process is made easier by using activities whose content is obviously a simulation of "real-world" concerns. When working with a group of persons in a laboratory setting, the task sometimes becomes so seductive that the group fails to look effectively at its own internal functioning. Such a process orientation can be generated rapidly by using an activity such as the checkerboard one to focus on interpersonal dynamics.

Processing. Perhaps our most firm commitment in laboratory design is to make absolutely certain that there is adequate time for processing the data that are generated by particular laboratory design components. It is in the processing activity itself, which immediately follows every learning experience, that the transfer of training is bolstered. If human relations training is, in fact, training for everyday work, then it is important that we heighten the probability that such transfer will take place. Processing refers to the talking through of behavioral and feeling data that emerge in a particular structured activity. We feel that is is both dangerous and unethical to leave large portions of data hanging that might be integrated in dysfunctional ways within the consciousness of a given individual. The importance of providing sufficient air time within the laboratory design to sort out and share reactions to particular events cannot be overemphasized. A number of structures have been developed to help participants to process data. The following is a partial compendium of these designs.

Participants and facilitators can be used as observers in particular structured experiences. It is sometimes useful to provide process-observation recording forms on which the observer may make notes during the event. Sometimes we may interrupt an event to hear reports from the process observers. Occasionally we have several process observers who form a discussion panel after the event to pool their observations. In laboratories, we often incorporate into the design the option for any number of participants to take turns functioning as external process observers. Occasionally we set up a particular structured experience in such a way that participants will stop at a predetermined point to process their reactions up to that point.

Facilitators may be used as consultants to a particular group that is accomplishing a task or working on a given problem within a laboratory. This may be done on a continuous basis—that is, a consultant may be brought in while a group is working on a particular problem—or the timing of the interventions of the process consultant may be preplanned. Laboratory participants also can be trained to perform this function.

After an activity on listening and process observation within a laboratory, participants can be encouraged to use each other as consultants in dyadic relationships that emerge during the laboratory. If two participants are having difficulty communicating with each other, they might seek out a third party to help them listen more effectively. This can be very useful training that can be transferred to the back-home situation. It is important for a participant to develop the ability to play the role of process consultant rather than to be a person who mediates conflict or takes sides on the content of a particular issue.

The group-on-group, or fishbowl, design is one of the most powerful processing designs with which we are familiar. What lends it potency is that the group operating within the fishbowl is under considerable pressure to work hard at focusing on process. In addition, the group can use other participants as consultants for its own internal functioning.

To increase the air time for any given participant it is often useful to break up a large group into a number of small units of three to six for rapid processing of data. Sometimes we structure this so that there are reporters who will give brief synopses to the total group at a predetermined time of the major themes that emerged in the subgroups. Subgrouping gives many people a chance to be heard and understood in less time, and it can heighten the getting-acquainted process.

A circle of chairs can be placed in the center of the room with the ground rule that if an individual wishes to speak about what is occurring he must occupy one of the chairs in the center. This has the effect of including, during any given period, any number of participants in open interchange, and it is particularly useful when working with very large groups of people.

In looking back at the process of learning in the laboratory experience, sometimes participants can focus on particular things that they have been doing by developing contracts, or promises, with each other that they attempt to fulfill in the time remaining. Sometimes this process of contracting can lead to highly useful applications in the back-home setting. We sometimes incorporate within the helping-pair design the writing of contracts for back-home application of the learning process that a particular person has been experiencing, with planned follow-through built into the contract.

Pacing. It is important for the facilitator to keep things moving and to avoid passivity and boredom, but he must be sensitive to the effects of fatigue on the participants. One can design a laboratory that has such a breakneck pace that participants come out of the event having been overloaded with stimuli. Some time is needed for people to think things out, and free time needs to be built in simply to give people an escape from the heavy work demands of a laboratory.

As a general rule, when things begin to drag, it is probably time to make a change. Sometimes the most effective change is simply to point up the process that is emerging and to help participants understand its nature. In a group meeting, for example, if there is a long silence, it may be important for the group to deal with the responsibility of the individual participants to avoid dysfunctional quiet. If the pace is characterized by frequent interventions on the part of the facilitator, it may lead to dependency on the part of the participants and they may come to expect him to make things happen. The pace of the events within a laboratory, then, should be dictated by the probable fatigue effect, the necessity to provide plenty of time for adequate processing of data, and the need not to reinforce dependency on the staff.

Goals. As has been previously indicated, it is critical for the facilitator to know the priorities and learning goals of a particular laboratory, to be able to specify them clearly, and to be able to keep the learning event goal-directed. It is important that he also be able to help participants clarify their own goals if they are somewhat unclear. Every person in the laboratory should have some understanding of why he is there.

Voluntariness. A major goal of laboratory education is to increase freedom rather than to co-opt people into activities in which they otherwise might not participate voluntarily. This is especially true if persons attend the laboratory involuntarily. Some persons react with a great deal of tension to activities involving physical touch, and they should not be required or unduly coerced to participate in such activities. The silent member of the intensive small group may be tyrannized by other group members into saying things that he does not want to reveal, and his voluntariness may be violated. Thus, in designing a laboratory, one must be sensitive to the needs of some participants not to involve themselves in every single activity.

Norms. The most meaningful expectations in the laboratory situation for the facilitator to establish and maintain are strategic openness, experimentation, and sensitivity to self and others. Strategic openness means avoiding the extremes of being dysfunctionally open or of colluding with other people not to talk about taboo topics. Experimentation means trying new behaviors within the laboratory situation. Sensitivity to self and others means that participants should be aware of the feelings that they are experiencing and that they should also attempt to be aware of the readiness of other people to get involved with them in open interchange of here-and-now data.

Data. Thoughts, feelings, and behavior are always present at any given point in the laboratory. Sometimes during a particular event participants may comment that nothing appears to be happening, but often this is simply evidence that they are not monitoring the complexity of the emerging process. The data-generating techniques that have been discussed previously can be highly effective in focusing particular here-and-now phenomena toward the learning goals of the laboratory.

Flexibility. The designer of the laboratory must plan to use maximum data from the event itself to modify the design so that it meets the learning needs of the participants. This means that he avoids "packaged" designs that are preplanned and that do not adequately account for the responsiveness of particular participants. We find it useful to overdesign laboratories in the sense that at any given point several options are being considered. This implies a lot of staffing time, especially if staff members are new to each other. In effect, this consideration of several options at any given point becomes a kind of on-the-job training for designing learning events.

SEQUENCING

There is, we believe, an organic sequence of activities that is useful to consider in designing human relations training laboratories. The attempt in this section is to delineate this sequence in terms of the laboratory components previously discussed. Although the emphasis is often different, the flow of activities within different kinds of learning programs overlaps somewhat. We will consider the design of two kinds of laboratories that are the most common types to be developed by group facilitators; the personal-growth laboratory and the leadership-development laboratory.

Personal Growth. The model for many personal growth laboratories has been the design, or lack of design, associated with two-week laboratories held in a retreat setting. Participants and staff would meet for the first time without an organized plan for activities, and together they would work through structuring a learning experience out of the ambiguities of an unstructured situation. A power vacuum would be artificially created by the phenomenon of the facilitators' refusal to accept responsibility for telling the participants what to do. The typical participant response would be a series of "plop" statements, such as "Why don't we introduce ourselves?" Long periods of silence would be experienced, and after the frustration created by the situation reached a significantly high level, the group would begin to focus with varying degrees of hostility on the trainers. The comments would then tend to be "What are we supposed to be doing here? If they're paying you, they're paying you too much." The net result of this was that the group members would eventually come to accept that they were responsible for their own learning. On the way to that awareness, they would have resolved their issues around the power vacuum. This would inevitably include issues about leadership expectations, and frequently the plethora of feeling about authority figures would be opened up and discussed.

Although the learnings inherent in dealing with the power vacuum were important, they consumed an inordinate amount of time when the design was translated to the weekend or weekly meeting models that have become more prevalent. Facilitators learned that what worked in a two-week design in the Maine woods does not necessarily work in a group that has a shorter lifetime. The training issue then becomes how to accelerate learning given restrictive time constraints. The use of structured experiences to focus on learning concepts, to generate learning data, and to accelerate the growth of group development and individual awareness signals the beginning of a set of solutions for the design dilemma.

In a personal growth laboratory, although there are definite learning goals that involve the use of skills in their accomplishment, there is less emphasis on skill building than there is in the leadership-development laboratory. The two key goals in personal growth are developing awareness of self and others and increasing skills in interpersonal relationships. Toward these ends, skills in listening, expressing, and responding are needed, and their development must be integrated into the design of the laboratory. These three skills will be discussed more thoroughly when an account of all the skills necessary for leadership development is made. This is one of the areas in which these two basic laboratory concepts overlap.

The sequence of events leading to the optimum use of time in fostering the learning goals in personal growth can be developed from the flow of learning that is implied in the following tabulation. The intent here is to spell out a series of things that need to be done in the laboratory in a logical flow, from getting acquainted to going home. This sequence is relevant both to retreats and to spaced meetings. A variety of structures can be utilized to effect this sequence. This is not the design of an ideal laboratory so much as it is an outline of the learning needs of participants during a personal growth laboratory.

1. *Getting Acquainted.* The major need at the beginning of the laboratory is for participants to establish some familiarity with one another, so that the initial caution with which people interact can be eased. The unfreezing process begins in the initial stages of the laboratory. A variety of getting-acquainted designs is available in the literature on structured experiences in human relations training.

2. *Closing Expectation Gaps.* It is important that the goals of the laboratory experience be made explicit and that they be correlated with the goals of participants. It is equally important that participants and staff have a clear understanding of what each expects of the other. The most difficult training situation that we know of exists when participants expect one kind of experience and staff members expect something else. Under this condition there needs to be immediate negotiation and clarification of assumptions.

3. *Legitimizing Risk Taking.* Early in the laboratory experience, it is significant for participants to test their willingness to know and to be known by other people, to express their feelings, to explore how other people are reacting to them, and to attempt new ways of behaving in relation to other people. At this point it is important that risk taking be legitimized and reinforced as a norm in the laboratory setting.

4. *Learning About Feedback.* Soon after the beginning of the laboratory experience, it is useful to provide some instruction about the feedback process so that effective sharing can be heightened in the intensive, small-group sessions and in the free time between formally planned sessions. Lecturettes, structured experiences, instruments, and trainer interventions can serve to provide an atmosphere in which feedback becomes expected and experienced freely. These methods can also introduce some conceptual models to guide participants in the sharing of information about one another.

5. *Developing an Awareness of Process.* After the intensive small group in a personal growth laboratory has had a brief history, it is often highly useful to begin to explore the dynamic processes that are emerging in the development of the group. This may be done through a fishbowl procedure or a variety of other designs previously discussed. The group can grow more rapidly if it stops occasionally in the interaction among members to process the patterns that are beginning to emerge in its development.

6. *Integrating Conceptual Models.* Transfer of training is more likely to be achieved if participants receive assistance in integrating the behavioral and affective data of the laboratory experience by looking at some theoretical models of personal and group development. This may be done through the use of instruments, lecturettes, demonstrations, and so on.

7. *Experimenting with Self-Expression.* Growth in awareness of self and others can be heightened through the use of expressive techniques such as nonverbal exercises and fantasies. Toward the middle of the laboratory experience, it is often useful to build into the design some opportunity for people to "stretch" their personal development through the use of symbolic self-expression.

8. *Planning Back-Home Application.* Ideally, plans for back-home application

begin to develop from the beginning of the laboratory. For example, an early experience that is often useful is a goal-setting activity, with reassessment in the middle and at the end of the laboratory. Often we use role playing, contracting, and helping pairs for applying learnings of the laboratory to particular back-home situations. Toward the end of the experience, considerable effort should be made toward getting participants to accept responsibility for making definite plans for changes that they want to institute after the laboratory is over. These plans need to be evaluated in the light of criteria for application, and this evaluation is often best done in collaboration with one or two other individuals with whom the participant feels comfortable.

9. *Assisting Re-Entry.* Closure activities in a personal growth laboratory should enable the participant to move back into his ordinary environment with a minimal amount of difficulty. Activities that emphasize feeling and cause participants to be "high" can result in dysfunctional re-entry into the immediate back-home situation. It is important to assist participants in exploring the observation that they are full of consciousness of themselves. At this point they are far more sensitive to their feelings and are more willing to be involved with people in open, trusting ways than are their "real-life" associates who have not just spent a considerable amount of time in a personal growth laboratory.

This general sequence does not imply a rigid structure. It is simply an attempt to highlight the needs of participants to develop an ability to talk with each other, to learn how to make sense out of the interaction that is occurring, and to heighten the development of ways that participants can use the experience in their everyday lives.

Leadership Development. Another genre of training events has been known by a number of euphemistic titles. One often sees labels such as "dynamics of leadership," "management development," "executive development," and "communication skills," and the events themselves are sometimes publicized as conferences, workshops, laboratories, or seminars. Thematic in these training events is a focus on skill building and conceptual development through experiential methods. They differ from personal growth laboratories more in degree than in kind; that is, there is a comparatively higher degree of emphasis on skill building and comparatively lower emphasis on growth in awareness of feelings about self and others. There is also a comparatively higher degree of structure within the design and a liberal use of simulations within the laboratory setting.

The skills that are learned during a leadership-development laboratory are multifarious. They include listening, expressing, responding, participating, collaborating, facilitating, observing, intervening, reporting, and conceptualizing. The skills that we will discuss first are the ones that receive the most attention in the laboratory; those toward the end receive comparatively less emphasis. This is, of course, a very subjective ranking of their importance within the training program.

Listening is a basic communication skill, and it is reinforced throughout the laboratory experience by means of structured activities and through the process of paraphrasing within intensive small-group meetings. Expressing one's thoughts and feelings is worked on through nonverbal exercises, through process-reporting exercises, through intensive group meetings, etc. Responding to the communication of others is the third basic communication skill that is reinforced during the leadership-development laboratory. The intent in working on this skill is for people to develop a heightened awareness of and sensitivity to the persons to whom they are responding, so that they are able to communicate within a system that has meaning to others.

Leaders need to know how to be followers because following is a part of leading. Participating in group activities in which the "leader" is simply one of a group of people working shoulder-to-shoulder is an important skill to focus on during the laboratory experience. In developing skill in collaborating, participants are encouraged to learn how to use conflict functionally and to avoid conflict-reducing techniques, e.g., horse-trading, in order to determine the best judgment of the group in solving problems. Leaders need to develop the ability to facilitate other people's growth by encouraging them to take responsibility for the task that faces the group. Some skill building is needed in defining leadership as the facilitation or sharing of responsibility.

When observing, leaders need to be able to see the complexity of intra-individual, interindividual, intragroup, and intergroup phenomena, so some skill development is planned within the laboratory to help leaders learn about the behavioral manifestations of interpersonal dynamics. Closely related to observing is the skill in using what one sees to help a group to improve its own internal functioning by learning about its ongoing process. Leaders need to develop the consultation skill of process intervention. In addition, leaders need skills in reporting or summarizing large batches of group content in order to provide succinct accounts of what has been decided.

Conceptualizing is perhaps the most complex of leadership skills. This involves looking at human interaction from a theoretical point of view. Conceptual models can be incorporated into leadership-development laboratories in such a way as to allow the leaders to develop their own theories of leadership.

The following sequence is, we believe, an organic, logical, and effective flow of activities that need to take place in leadership-development laboratories. Again, this sequence is proposed as relevant whether the laboratory takes place over a weekend or during a semester-long course.

1. *Getting Acquainted.* Here the basic need is to infuse a note of psychological safety into the proceedings by familiarizing participants with each other and with staff members on a personal level. The effort is to create a climate in which people can have easy access to each other. It is important in the beginning of such laboratories for people to be able to establish their credentials. Often participants feel a strong need to impress people with who and what they are.

2. *Closing Expectation Gaps.* In a leadership-development laboratory, as in a personal growth laboratory, it is important that the goals of the laboratory experience be made explicit and correlated with the goals of participants. It is equally important that participants and staff have a clear understanding of what each expects of the other. If the facilitator determines that there is a wide expectation gap, he must immediately negotiate to close it.

3. *Roles and Shared Leadership.* The concept of roles and functions of different

group members and the notion of dynamic, shared leadership is introduced. This sets the tone for using theoretical material in an experiential format to focus on ourselves as leaders in relation to other people.

4. *Learning About Feedback.* Soon after the beginning of the laboratory experience, it is useful to provide instruction in the feedback process so that effective sharing can be increased. Lecturettes, structured activities, instruments, and trainer interventions can serve to provide an atmosphere in which feedback becomes expected and experienced freely.

5. *Developing an Awareness of Process.* After the leadership-development laboratory has had a brief history, it is highly useful to begin to explore the dynamic processes emerging in the group. This may be done through a fishbowl procedure or a variety of other designs previously discussed. The group can develop effectively if it stops occasionally in the interaction among members to process the kinds of leadership and roles that are beginning to emerge.

6. *Competition Task.* Early in a leadership-development laboratory, we introduce an activity that is likely to result in participants' exploring the functional and dysfunctional effects of interpersonal competition. Sometimes a competitive atmosphere is established deliberately, such as in an intergroup model-building activity, or it may arise spontaneously in a relatively unstructured task experience.

7. *Collaboration Task.* It is useful to follow a competitive experience with an activity in which people are expected to attempt deliberately to collaborate with other people on a task. The aim is to demonstrate that collaboration is possible within a culture that rewards competitive spirit.

8. *Consensus Task.* Closely related to the collaboration task is consensus seeking. Many structured experiences can be chosen from the point of view of involving a number of people in arriving at collective judgments that are superior to individual judgments. What we attempt to illustrate in this kind of experience is the concept of synergy.

9. *Planning Back-Home Application.* Toward the end of the laboratory experience it is important for the participants to begin making definite plans for particular behaviors that they want to experiment with and/or change in their back-home leadership situations. It is sometimes useful to have participants write themselves letters about what they are going to attempt to change, based on both cognitive material and their own experiences during the laboratory.

In addition to a sequence of activities fostering skill building and the development of a set of leadership concepts, some material is thematic throughout a leadership-development laboratory design. Three concepts need to be stressed during the laboratory itself: process awareness, criteria of effective feedback, and theories of leadership. The design of the leadership-development laboratory in general, then, consists of encouraging participants to experiment with leadership phenomena, involving them in a series of activities to explore leadership from the point of view of looking at themselves in roles, exploring group effects and the dynamics of competition and collaboration, and planning the transfer of learning to the leadership situation back home.

PROFESSIONAL DEVELOPMENT IN DESIGNING LABORATORIES

Building a Repertoire. A number of steps can be taken to improve one's ability to design training laboratories. A first step in developing such skill is to build a repertoire of materials that can be used in design work. The facilitator can become familiar with structured experiences and instruments available for use in training and can master an array of lecture materials that he can call on at a moment's notice to explain particular phenomena in the laboratory setting.

Co-Facilitating. A second step in improving the ability to design laboratories is to be active in seeking opportunities to work with a variety of other facilitators. This has a number of important advantages. One can receive concentrated, highly specific feedback on one's style as a facilitator, can improve one's ability to diagnose participants' needs, and can spend staff time critiquing the design and debriefing laboratories after they are completed. This, we believe, is the best professional-development strategy that is currently available. There is no substitute for experience with other trained professionals working in a laboratory setting with live participants.

Varying Clients. A third step that the facilitator can take is to seek out opportunities to work with various client groups. This requires that the facilitator be flexible in design and avoid developing design packages that may be irrelevant to the learning needs of particular clients. There are obvious ethical restrictions on the facilitator as he seeks out clients. Since human relations training is generally considered to be a professional-level activity, professional ethics require that the facilitator not over-represent his qualifications. But within ethical restrictions, he can grow professionally by generating experience in working with a variety of participants.

Studying Designs. Another activity that can result in professional development in designing laboratories is to study other facilitators' designs. This is a somewhat controversial subject in that, within the field of laboratory education, there is a tendency for facilitators to be closed and possessive about the designs they have developed. It is not uncommon for facilitators to conclude that they have developed a program that is highly salable, and one often encounters reluctance to share designs with other professionals. What has happened within this field, then, is the systematic violation of a norm that we try to sell to clients: to be open and collaborative. University Associates conducted a life-planning laboratory some time ago in which over half the participants attended primarily to learn how to conduct the laboratory themselves. We renamed the event the "rip-off lab," and we had a good laugh about it. What was significant about the experience was the fact that before the laboratory began the participants' hidden agenda was a taboo topic. We made it an open subject and legitimized it so that people would not feel the need to conceal their motives from the laboratory staff. In studying other facilitators' designs, however, it is important that the design not be accepted *in toto*. Others' designs are almost always, in some aspect, irrelevant to the particular needs of another client system. Adaptation should be the keynote.

Attending Workshops. A fifth step that the group facilitator can take to develop himself in the area of design is to attend professional-development workshops. Many learning experiences are available for the behavioral-science consultant that afford opportunities to obtain supervised practice in the design of laboratories. Various training organizations, such as National Training Laboratories and University Associates, offer such professional-development programs.

Attending Labs as a Participant. Finally, it is highly useful for the facilitator to attend laboratories occasionally as a participant rather than as a staff member. The human element is the critical point in effective facilitation. The most significant ethical boundary impinging on the facilitator is the need to remain healthy: not to deceive himself about who he is, what he is up to, where he is going, and so on. Experiencing laboratories as a participant means living by the same kind of values that we are attempting to teach other people and continuing to develop our ability to provide experiences that offer meaningful human contact with other people. The major need in staff development is to integrate one's personal and professional development. Personal growth is necessary but not sufficient; even though the facilitator may be a highly effective person, he still needs the technology of laboratory education in order to be effective in fostering other people's development.

We have attempted in this paper to spell out some of the learnings about the process of designing laboratories for the enhancement of personal growth and leadership development so that facilitators can explore this task more straightforwardly and creatively. We continue to stress the norm that such ideas be shared by facilitators in the field.

REFERENCES

Blake, R., & Mouton, J. S. The instrumented training laboratory. In I. R. Weschler & E. M. Schein (Eds.), *Selected readings series five: Issues in training.* Washington, DC: National Training Laboratories, 1962, pp. 61-85.

Buchanan, P. C., & Reisel, J. Differentiating human relations training laboratories. *Social Changes,* 1972, *2,* 1-3.

Jones, J. E. Types of growth groups. In J. W. Pfeiffer & J. E. Jones (Eds.), *The 1972 annual handbook for group facilitators.* San Diego, CA: University Associates, 1972.

Pfeiffer, J. W., & Jones, J. E. (Eds.). *A handbook of structured experiences for human relations training* (Vols. I, II, III, IV, V, VI, VII, and VIII). San Diego, CA: University Associates, 1969 & 1974; 1970 & 1974; 1971 & 1974; 1973; 1975; 1977; 1979; 1981.

INTRODUCTION TO STRUCTURED EXPERIENCES

Structured experiences—designed to focus on individual behavior, constructive feedback, processing, and psychological integration—are infinitely varied and variable. They can be adapted easily to the particular needs of the group, the aim of a training design, or the special competencies of the facilitator. In publishing structured experiences, we assume that facilitators are, by their nature, innovators. As one friend remarked, "I use your materials all the time, but I almost never do things the way you guys describe them."

Since the expertise of individual facilitators varies, we have arranged the structured experiences in the *Annuals* and the *Handbooks* in order of the degree of understanding, skill, and experience required by the facilitator. The first structured experiences generate less affect and data than do later ones, thus demanding much less background of the facilitator to use them effectively and responsibly.

We are concerned that all human relations training experiences have adequate processing so that the participants are able to integrate their learning without the stress generated by unresolved feelings or a lack of understanding. It is here that the expertise of the facilitator becomes crucial. If the structured experience is to be responsive to the needs of the participants, the facilitator must be able to assist the participants in successfully processing the data that emerge from that experience. Thus, an activity should be selected on the basis of two criteria—the facilitator's competence and the participants' needs.

CONSIDERATIONS IN DEVELOPING A STRUCTURED EXPERIENCE

To further the creation and availability of these valuable materials, we are including some points and questions to be considered when developing a structured experience.

Goals. These should be limited in number and stated in language that participants can understand. A good goal is *specific* in that it states exactly what will occur; it is less specific in terms of the result of that occurrence, in order to permit *inductive* learning, i.e., learning through discovery. For example, a goal may be "to examine" or "to explore" the effects of collaboration and competition. The activity will involve those two dynamics. What is learned, however, may differ from participant to participant, depending on their backgrounds and their unique experiences during the activity. A goal is *performance oriented,* to guide the person toward what he is going to *do*; it *involves* the individual in his goal objective; it is *observable,* so that other people can see the result; and, most important, it is *realistic.* For maximum effectiveness, a goal must be attainable.

Group Size. The minimum and maximum number of participants, the optimum size of the group, and the number and size of subgroups should be noted where relevant. If there are extra participants, how should they be utilized? (They could, for example, be designated as observers or added to subgroups.)

Time Required. This should be a realistic expectation, based on actual trials of the experience. Adequate time must be allowed for sharing and processing the learnings. If the experience requires a long period of time, can it be divided into more than one session?

Materials. The criteria here are easy availability, utility, and uncomplicated preparation. The specific forms, sheets of information, or work sheets needed and the quantities of each should be listed. If appropriate, an observer sheet should be devised for the activity. Audiovisual aids (such as felt-tipped pens, newsprint, sound or film equipment), pencils and paper, and any other special materials should be indicated if applicable.

Physical Setting. What are the participants' needs: Must groups be private, quiet, isolated? Do participants sit around tables or lie on the floor? Do they need writing surfaces? Can the experience take place outdoors? Do rooms need to be specially designated or arranged for certain groups or subgroups? Easily movable furniture is usually desirable to aid in the flexibility of the group.

Process. This is a step-by-step procedure that should indicate what the facilitator *does* and *says* and what the participants *do* in the appropriate sequence. The beginning and end of each step should be specified. A time estimate may be useful for each step or phase.

Variations. Adaptations may be noted to vary the activity's content, sequence, use of observers, time for each step, materials, size of groups, complexity of process, and use with intact groups.

References. If and when relevant, similar structured experiences, lecturette sources, or background reading should be indicated.

Credit Line. Ideas and designs of others should be acknowledged; if there is more than one author to be credited, the authors' names should appear in the order of the significance of their contributions, the senior author or contributor listed first.

Work Sheets. These should be designed and written so that they contain sufficient room in which the participants may write; are simple and easy to reproduce; have clear instructions; and are necessary and meaningful to the activity. Whenever possible, each work sheet should be on one page, with type large enough to read easily. It is practical to have the work sheet contain its own instructions. If it does not, it should tell the participant that the facilitator will give oral instructions. Sources for work sheets should be acknowledged.

Handouts. This format is especially useful for a discussion of the theory underlying new behavior suggested by the structured experience. Unless necessary, participants should not be allowed to read handout materials while the process is running. However, if handouts are to be provided, the participants should be told at the beginning of the experience so that they will not prepare to take notes.

CONSIDERATIONS IN USING A STRUCTURED EXPERIENCE

Certain questions need to be asked by the facilitator who is contemplating using a structured experience as an intervention in a training event. This set of considerations constitutes a self-examination that is intended to help the facilitator select and develop designs that are both relevant and effective.

What are the goals of this group and why was it formed? Structured experiences are designed for a variety of purposes, but their most effective use is within programs that are aimed at specific learning goals. The facilitator needs to keep these goals in mind constantly.

At what stage is the group in its development or what stage is it likely to reach? Different issues surface at various stages of group development, and some activities are particularly useful at some points in group life. A feedback design may be inappropriate in the earliest stages but highly beneficial after the group has a brief history.

What is my contract with the group? Some groups expect the facilitator to "run" everything. It is important to minimize the gap in expectations between the facilitator and the participants. Using too many structured experiences may reinforce dependency on the part of the members, and they may turn to the facilitator to introduce an activity rather than confronting their own behavior. The facilitator needs to make it clear that each member is responsible for his own learning.

Why is it important that I intervene? Because it is possible for the facilitator to meet his own needs at the participants' expense, it is important that he assess his own motives for intervening into the interaction among members. Useful distinctions can be made between making things happen, letting things happen, and being a part of what is happening. One useful thought is "When in doubt, wait."

Why does this particular intervention appeal to me? It may be that the structured experience seems appropriate because it would be "fun" to do, but the overriding consideration should be the learning needs of the participants at a particular point in the group's development. One should be careful not to overuse any given activity; this might indicate that the facilitator has "a solution in search of a problem."

How ready are these participants to take risks, to experiment? Some structured experiences, such as guided fantasies and nonverbal activities, are threatening to many participants and may evoke anxiety and defensiveness rather than openness to learning. It is useful, however, to establish an experimentation norm in laboratory education, and participants should be expected to "stretch" somewhat.

What content modifications can I make for an effective, appealing design? Local issues and concerns can be incorporated into structured-experience materials and processes in order to heighten the possibility of the transfer of training. Such advance preparation can have a high payoff in developing work norms and avoiding "game playing." Roles, goals, company policies, issues, cases, etc., can be gathered with the help of participants.

What advance preparations need to be made? Appropriate rooms, with the right kinds of furniture and equipment, need to be scheduled. The staff may need to be prepared. Materials have to be duplicated and assembled. Sometimes it is helpful to prearrange the furniture so that participants are seated in preparation for the first phase of the process.

How rigid are the time restraints for the session? It is necessary not to generate more data than can be adequately processed within the session. It is better not to use an activity than to leave too much data "hanging" at the end. One consideration is to anticipate which elements of the design can be speeded up or expanded, if necessary.

How am I going to set up the processing? Since the processing of the data generated by the structured experience is more important than the experience itself, this planning phase should be carefully considered. A number of strategies can be used, such as process observers who have been briefed and who are using comprehensive guides; lecturettes; instrumented processing with brief questionnaires; subgrouping; the empty chair or group-on-group techniques; and interviewing. Some of the data may be saved for use in later training designs.

How am I going to evaluate the effectiveness of the design? Since structured experiences are best employed in an atmosphere directed toward specific goals, some assessment of the extent to which the goals of a given activity were met is necessary. Such a study may be impressionistic and/or "objective," but it needs to be planned beforehand. The facilitator needs to decide the basis for judging whether or not or to what degree the aims of a particular intervention were accomplished.

FAILURE OF STRUCTURED EXPERIENCES

Structured experiences can "fail." That is, they may not produce the predicted results, or they may produce unexpected results.

Usually, such failure occurs when the experiential model is truncated or abbreviated or when it is inadequately implemented. Each step in the model is an essential part of the entire sequence; each needs sufficient attention to effect its full impact. Inadequate processing is the most common cause of the failure of the model.

Unfortunately, failure on the part of any facilitator only increases the chances that other facilitators may encounter difficulty in their attempts to present a structured experience. If participants in a learning activity have previously had ineffective training experiences, it is likely that they will be more resistant to, and less inclined to involve themselves in, such experiences in the future.

Thus, the question of the "failure" of structured experiences becomes significant. Failure promotes subsequent failure. For this reason, we are stressing here the need for facilitators to confront the demands and requirements of the experiential model so that they—and their colleagues who follow them—may gather the rewards and benefits the model offers.

The implications of the model stress the necessity for adequate planning and sufficient time for each step. An appropriate structure is especially important for processing, generalizing, and applying. When handled with care, concern, and skill, the experiential approach is invaluable for group facilitators in the human relations training field.

NUMBERING OF STRUCTURED EXPERIENCES

The structured experiences are numbered consecutively throughout the series of *Handbooks* and *Annuals*, in order of publication of the volumes. The following list specifies the numbers of the structured experiences to be found in each publication in the Pfeiffer and Jones Series in Human Relations Training.

Structured Experience	Publication
1 through 24	Volume I, *Handbook*
25 through 48	Volume II, *Handbook*
49 through 74	Volume III, *Handbook*
75 through 86	1972 *Annual*
87 through 100	1973 *Annual*
101 through 124	Volume IV, *Handbook*
125 through 136	1974 *Annual*
137 through 148	1975 *Annual*
149 through 172	Volume V, *Handbook*
173 through 184	1976 *Annual*
185 through 196	1977 *Annual*
197 through 220	Volume VI, *Handbook*
221 through 232	1978 *Annual*
233 through 244	1979 *Annual*
245 through 268	Volume VII, *Handbook*
269 through 280	1980 *Annual*
281 through 292	1981 *Annual*
293 through 316	Volume VIII, *Handbook*

CLASSIFICATION OF STRUCTURED EXPERIENCES

THE NEW FORMAT

Professionals who use the structured experiences in the *Handbooks* and *Annuals* have long sought any easy, reliable way to choose appropriate activities for particular training events. To meet this need, we have reclassified[1] the 316 structured experiences in this *Reference Guide*—all the structured experiences previously published in the eight volumes of *A Handbook of Structured Experiences for Human Relations Training* and the ten volumes of *The Annual Handbook for Group Facilitators*—into the following six major categories, based on the *goals* of the experience:

- Personal: activities that focus on the expansion of personal insight, awareness, and development of interpersonal skills.

- Communication: activities that emphasize verbal and nonverbal communication skills, especially in interpersonal and intragroup relationships.

- Group Characteristics: activities that examine how individuals affect group functioning.

- Group Task Behavior: activities that focus on how groups organize and function to accomplish objectives.

- Organizations: activities that help individuals and groups function within an organizational context.

- Facilitating Learning: activities that create a climate of responsiveness and encourage skill development.

Each major category has been divided into subcategories in order to help the trainer select activities with a high degree of precision. The same subcategories may be included under more than one major category, e.g., "values clarification" is under "Personal" and under "Group Characteristics." Of course, structured experiences may be used for any number of goals other than those indicated, but by using this categorization, the professional trainer will greatly increase the likelihood of finding experiences that have been designed to meet his or her particular goals. It is true that a sophisticated classification system necessarily involves fine distinctions about the placement of a particular activity. The primary intent of this system is to help the user find materials quickly and with discrimination. We support and encourage facilitators in developing their own cross-reference systems for the use of activities.

Definitions of the subcategory topics within major categories follow.

---

[1]We would like to acknowledge the contributions of Peter Rutherford to the conception and planning of the new category system.

Personal

Self-Disclosure: activities that teach the ability to reveal oneself to others.

Sensory: activities that focus on personal awareness and skills through the exploration of the senses.

Feelings Awareness: experiences that focus on emotional understanding of oneself.

Feedback: activities that promote awareness of others' ability to increase one's understanding of self and that encourage acceptance of the opinions or feelings of others.

Assumptions: activities that help one to see that the assumptions he or she may make about others may significantly influence perceptions.

Values Clarification: activities that clarify the process by which one chooses, prizes, or acts.

Life/Career Planning: activities that allow one to evaluate the present and future of one's career or life.

Communication

Communication Awareness Experiments: activities that illustrate what happens when two people communicate, either verbally or nonverbally.

Developing Interpersonal Trust in Dyads: activities that help two people to develop a personal or work relationship.

Sexual Awareness: experiences that expand awareness of and skill in handling the sexual aspect of relationships.

Listening: skill-building activities that help people to listen actively.

Interviewing: activities to develop skills needed in the two-person interview situation.

Assertion: activities that improve people's ability to affirm their own positions while being sensitive to the needs of others.

Group Characteristics

Process Observation/Awareness: activities that help to develop skills in observing what is taking place in a group.

Leadership-Membership: activities that deal with issues of power, leadership style, motivation, and leaders' and members' interactions with each other.

Communication: activities that offer practice in group communication.

Values Clarification/Stereotyping: activities to illustrate the effects *on the group* of individuals' personal values and their stereotypes or prejudices.

Group Task Behavior

Problem Solving/Awareness: activities that develop skill in and awareness of problem-solving techniques.

Generating Alternatives: activities to practice an early creative step of the problem-solving process.

Group Feedback: activities that develop awareness of and skills in group feedback.

Competition (Win-Lose): activities that involve competitive behavior by group members and explore its effect on the accomplishment of a task.

Competition and Collaboration (Win-Lose and Win-Win): activities that deal both with the competitive tendencies that emerge within groups and the appropriateness of collaborative behavior.

Collaboration (Win-Win): activities that deal with only the cooperative aspect of group task behavior.

Conflict Resolution/Values Polarization: activities that develop skills to deal with conflicts in the group because of differing values of members.

Consensus/Synergy: activities to develop the group's skills at reaching general agreement and commitment to its decisions and goals.

Organizations

Awareness/Diagnosis: activities that help people to be aware of the forces that affect the functioning of their organizations and to learn to diagnose organizational problems.

Team Building: learning experiences to develop the effectiveness of teams within an organization.

Decision Making/Action Planning: activities that teach these necessary skills within organizations.

Conflict Resolution/Values: activities that look at values within the organizational context and at conflicts caused by differences between personal values and organizational values.

Consultation Skills: experiences that develop the skill of the internal or external consultant.

Facilitating Learning

Getting Acquainted: activities designed for warming up a learning group that is meeting for the first time.

Forming Subgroups: activities that help a newly formed learning group break into subgroups for learning purposes.

Expectations of Learners/Facilitators: activities for use when a gap potentially exists between what the learners expect and what the facilitator is offering.

Dealing with Blocks to Learning: activities developed to deal with situations in which learning is blocked through the interference of other dynamics, conscious or unconscious, in the group.

Building Trust: activities to create trust and a climate of openness and learning within the group.

Building Norms of Openness: activities that help group participants expand their learning by being willing to give and receive feedback.

Energizers: activities that "recharge" the group when energy is low.

Evaluating Learning-Group Process: activities to help individuals evaluate what is taking place within a learning group.

Developing Group Facilitator Skills: activities designed to develop the abilities of trainers, group leaders, or group facilitators.

Closure: activities to use at the end of a training event.

Classifying these materials is somewhat arbitrary, since they can be adapted for a variety of training purposes. Although any given experience could belong to a number of classifications, we have listed each only once, categorizing it in the area of its *most probable* use.

PERSONAL
Self-Disclosure

Number	Title [Author]	Goals	Time Required	Volume & Page No.
16	**Fantasies:** Suggestions for Individuals and Groups	To promote heightened awareness of self and others	Varies with each fantasy	I-75
20	**Graphics:** Self-Disclosure Activities	To generate self-disclosure data through graphics	Varies with each activity	I-88

Sensory

Number	Title [Author]	Goals	Time Required	Volume & Page No.
19	**Awareness Expansion:** A Potpourri	To heighten one's sensory awareness	Varies with each activity	I-86
71	**Lemons:** A Sensory-Awareness Activity	To increase sensory awareness	One hour	III-94
136	**Relaxation and Perceptual Awareness:** A Workshop [J.L. Hipple, M. Hutchins, & J. Barott]	To learn basic techniques of physical relaxation, breathing processes, and self-awareness. To experience one's physical state of existence and personal perceptions of inner and outer reality and fantasy	Three hours	'74-84
199	**T'ai Chi Chuan:** An Introduction to Movement Awareness [D.X. Swenson]	To increase body self-awareness. To develop integrated, relaxed, economical, and balanced movement and activity. To facilitate a feeling of "centeredness" in the here-and-now	Approximately one hour	VI-10

Feelings Awareness

Number	Title [Author]	Goals	Time Required	Volume & Page No.
56	**Feelings and Defenses:** A Spontaneous Lecture	To study feelings significant to group members and defenses they use. To help group members take responsibility for their own learning	About thirty minutes	III-31
65	**Think-Feel:** A Verbal Progression [J.E. Jones]	To make distinctions between thoughts and feelings. To learn to link feeling feedback to observable behavior. To practice empathizing	Forty-five minutes	III-70

Feelings Awareness (Continued)

Number	Title [Author]	Goals	Time Required	Volume & Page No.
75	**Frustrations and Tensions**	To help participants to become aware of their responses to tense, frustrating situations. To study alternative responses to such situations	Approximately forty-five minutes	'72-5
119	**Group Exploration:** A Guided Fantasy [L. Berman]	To allow individuals to share their means of coping with fear and stress as well as their personal responses to pleasure	Approximately one hour	IV-92
122	**Expressing Anger:** A Self-Disclosure Exercise [G.R. Gemmill]	To study styles of expressing anger in a group setting. To study effects of anger in a group setting. To legitimize the presence and expression of anger within groups. To identify behaviors which elicit anger in others. To explore ways of coping with anger	Approximately forty-five minutes	IV-104
300	**Projections:** Interpersonal Awareness Expansion [B. Nisenholz]	To help participants to explore the process of projection. To provide an opportunity for participants to recognize how and what they project about others. To enable participants to become more aware of the part they play in the outcome of unpleasant situations	One and one-half hours	VIII-30

Feedback

Number	Title [Author]	Goals	Time Required	Volume & Page No.
13	Johari Window: An Experience in Self-Disclosure and Feedback	To introduce the concept of the Johari Window. To permit participants to process data about themselves in terms of self-disclosure and feedback	Approximately two hours	I-65
23	Coins: Symbolic Feedback [J.W. Pfeiffer]	To experiment with giving feedback symbolically. To share feelings involved with giving, receiving, and rejection	Approximately one and one-half hours	I-104
58	Peer Perceptions: A Feedback Experience [J.E. Jones]	To let each group member know to what degree he is seen to be similar to each other member. To study feeling reactions to being considered "different." To help each member define the dimensions of human similarity and dissimilarity he believes are important	Two to three hours	III-41
97	Puzzlement: A "Mild" Confrontation [R.R. Kurtz]	To help participants confront each other's behavior in helpful ways. To stimulate the amount of feedback given and received in a group. To share the feelings involved in giving and receiving feedback	Approximately one and one-half hours	'73-30
99	Analyzing and Increasing Open Behavior: The Johari Window [P.G. Hanson]	To describe open and closed behavior in terms of the Johari Window. To identify facilitating and inhibiting forces which affect the exchange of feedback. To encourage the development of increased open behavior in the group through facilitated feedback	Approximately two and one-half hours	'73-38

Feedback (Continued)

Number	Title [Author]	Goals	Time Required	Volume & Page No.
107	**The Portrait Game:** Individual Feedback [F. Maire]	To allow participants to receive a composite feedback picture from the members of their group as a departure from single-source individual feedback. To provide an opportunity for participants to compare their individual perceptions of how the group is experiencing their behavior with the reality of the group's experience	A minimum of twenty minutes per participant	IV-24
123	**Stretching:** Identifying and Taking Risks [R.R. Kurtz]	To help participants become aware of interpersonal behavior which is risky for them. To increase participants' awareness of the relationship between risk-taking behavior and the attainment of personal growth goals. To encourage risk-taking behavior as a way of expanding participants' behavioral repertoire	Approximately two hours	IV-107
146	**Payday:** A Closure Activity [R.L. Bunning]	To provide for self- and group evaluation of each participant's performance within the group. To allow each participant to compare his self-evaluation with the group's evaluation of him. To give participants experience in evaluating others in a constructive, concrete manner	Approximately one hour	'75-54
168	**Adjectives:** Feedback [J.E. Jones]	To help participants clarify values that apply to human relationships. To establish the norms of soliciting and giving both positive and negative feedback	Approximately one hour	V-114

Feedback (Continued)

Number	Title [Author]	Goals	Time Required	Volume & Page No.
170	**Person Perception:** Feedback [R.H. Dolliver]	To provide feedback to individual group members about how they are perceived by others. To help participants clarify what underlies their tendency to categorize other persons	Approximately one hour	V-131
198	**Choose an Object:** A Getting-Acquainted Activity [D.L. Thompson]	To increase perception of oneself. To provide an opportunity to share personal perceptions. To provide an opportunity to receive feedback on perceived behavior	Approximately two hours	VI-7
209	**Introspection:** Personal Evaluation and Feedback [D.L. Smith]	To provide an opportunity for participants to compare their self-assessments with those of others	Approximately forty-five minutes	VI-57
216	**Affirmation of Trust:** A Feedback Activity [B.P. Holleran]	To increase understanding of physical, intellectual, and emotional trust. To explore how the trust level existing in the group affects the openness of discussion. To provide an opportunity for group members to give each other feedback on trust	Approximately two hours	VI-110
225	**Cards:** Personal Feedback [J.R. Luthi]	To encourage the exchange of personal feedback. To provide a means for giving and receiving personal feedback	Approximately two hours	'78-34

Feedback (Continued)

Number	Title [Author]	Goals	Time Required	Volume & Page No.
303	**Developing Trust:** A Leadership Skill [W.J. Bailey]	To examine some of the behaviors and personal qualities that affect the process of establishing trust in relationships. To analyze current behaviors and attitudes related to establishing trust in relationships. To increase awareness of how one is perceived by others in regard to behaviors that enhance the building of trust	Approximately two hours	VIII-45
315	**Giving and Receiving Feedback:** Contracting for New Behavior [J.E. Jones]	To provide an opportunity for members of a personal-growth group to give and receive feedback on their in-group behavior. To enable participants to set behavioral goals for the remainder of the group experience	Approximately three hours	VIII-125

Assumptions

Number	Title [Author]	Goals	Time Required	Volume & Page No.
213	**Sherlock:** An Inference Activity [R. Roskin]	To increase awareness of how prejudices, assumptions, and self-concepts influence perceptions and decisions. To explore the relationship between observation, knowledge, and inference. To help participants become aware of their personal preconceptions and biases	Approximately one and one-half hours	VI-92
227	**Young/Old Woman:** A Perception Experiment [W.R. Mulford]	To focus on individual reactions to the same stimulus. To examine the effects of the immediate environment on an individual's perception	Fifty minutes	'78-40

Assumptions (Continued)

Number	Title [Author]	Goals	Time Required	Volume & Page No.
229	**Pygmalion:** Clarifying Personal Biases [R.L. Bunning]	To discover how pre-conceived ideas may influence collective and/or individual actions. To allow participants to assess their current behavior in terms of previous "scripting" and social pressure	Approximately forty-five minutes	'78-51
247	**Prejudice:** An Awareness-Expansion Activity [R. Raine]	To share feelings and ideas about prejudices in a non-threatening manner. To explore the validity of common prejudices	One to one and one-half hours	VII-15
273	**Managerial Characteristics:** Exploring Stereotypes [A.K. Gulezian]	To increase awareness of masculine and feminine characteristics typically associated with effective managerial performance. To examine the male-manager stereotype and its implications for women in management. To provide an opportunity to examine self-perceptions relating to the concept of masculinity/femininity	One and one-half to two hours	'80-31
292	**Data Survey:** Exploring Stereotypes [T.J. Mulhern & M.A. Parashkevov]	To discover how one makes judgments about others on the basis of age, race, sex, or ethnic stereotypes. To provide an opportunity to examine personal reactions to the issue of prejudice	Approximately one and one-half hours	'81-57
305	**Sexism in Advertisements:** Exploring Stereotypes [A.J. Burr, D.C.L. Griffith, D.B. Lyon, G.E. Philpot, G.N. Powell, & D.L. Sehring]	To become more aware of sex-role stereotyping in advertisements. To identify elements of advertisements that do or do not reflect sex-role stereotyping. To increase awareness of the effects of social conditioning	Approximately one and one-half hours	VIII-58

Values Clarification

Number	Title [Author]	Goals	Time Required	Volume & Page No.
143	**Ideal Cards:** A Self-Disclosure Activity [B.P. Holleran]	To encourage interaction and self-disclosure about ideals. To reveal group members' priorities for their ideals	Approximately one and one-half hours	'75-43
233	**Banners:** A Value-Clarification Activity [M.A. Graham]	To increase self-understanding and self-awareness of values, goals, and individual potential. To provide a forum for the public expression of personal values, potentials, and goal-achievement standards. To examine how life values, potential, and goal achievement affect decisions concerning personal needs and aspirations	Two to three hours	'79-9
261	**Wants Bombardment:** A Psychosynthesis Activity [J.E. Jones]	To increase awareness of competing wants in one's life situation. To attempt to prioritize and/or synthesize one's wants	Approximately one and one-half hours	VII-105
283	**Louisa's Problem:** Value Clarification [C.E. Amesley]	To provide practice in clarifying issues and identifying values without passing judgment. To develop awareness of some of the factors affecting one's own value judgments and those of others. To provide an opportunity to exchange various points of view on a highly emotional issue	Approximately two hours	'81-13

Values Clarification (Continued)

Number	Title [Author]	Goals	Time Required	Volume & Page No.
298	Lifeline: A Value-Clarification Activity [S.H. Wyant]	To increase awareness of social influences on the formation of attitudes, beliefs, values, and perceptions. To examine personal development and growth in the context of political history, social movements, and popular culture. To share differing values and orientations	One and one-half hours	VIII-21

Life/Career Planning

Number	Title [Author]	Goals	Time Required	Volume & Page No.
46	Life Planning: A Programmed Approach	To apply concepts of planned change to an individual's personal, interpersonal, and career development	Six hours split into three two-hour periods	II-101
137	What Do You See? A Discovery Activity [A.G. Kirn]	To expand awareness of those things that have meaning for life and work. To discover new areas of individual relevance and interest. To promote changing negative thinking to positive thinking	A minimum of one hour	'75-7

COMMUNICATION
Communication Awareness Experiments (Oral)

Number	Title [Author]	Goals	Time Required	Volume & Page No.
4	One-Way, Two-Way: A Communications Experiment [adapted from H.J. Leavitt]	To conceptualize the superior functioning of two-way communication through participatory demonstration. To examine the application of communication in family, social, and occupational settings	Approximately forty-five minutes	I-13

Communication Awareness Experiments (Oral) (Continued)

Number	Title [Author]	Goals	Time Required	Volume & Page No.
28	**Rumor Clinic:** A Communications Experiment	To illustrate distortions which may occur in transmission of information from an original source through several individuals to a final destination	Thirty minutes	II-12
108	**Ball Game:** Controlling and Influencing Communication [R.D. Jorgenson]	To explore the dynamics of assuming leadership in a group. To increase awareness of the power held by the member of a group who is speaking at any given time. To diagnose communication patterns in a group	Approximately thirty minutes	IV-27
128	**Re-Owning:** Increasing Behavioral Alternatives [H.B. Karp]	To assist participants in exploring aspects of themselves that they might not be presently aware of or may be under-utilizing. To extend the range of behavioral alternatives open for effective communication	Approximately one hour	'74-18
202	**Dominoes:** A Communication Experiment [S.H. Putnam]	To enhance awareness of factors that help or hinder effective interpersonal communication. To explore the effect on task-oriented behavior of shared versus unshared responsibility	Approximately one and one-half hours	VI-21
241	**Blivet:** A Communication Experience [K. Myers, R. Tandon, & H. Bowens, Jr.]	To demonstrate and experience one-way and two-way verbal communication. To demonstrate and experience barriers and aids to verbal communication. To explore the effects of different status positions on interpersonal communication	Approximately one and one-half hours	'79-46

Communication Awareness Experiments (Oral) (Continued)

Number	Title [Author]	Goals	Time Required	Volume & Page No.
250	**Meanings Are in People:** Perception Checking [J.N. Wismer]	To demonstrate that meanings are not in words but in the people who use them and hear them. To illustrate that our perceptions of words attribute positive, neutral, and negative meanings to them	One to three hours	VII-28
251	**Mixed Messages:** A Communication Experiment [B.K. Holmberg & D.W. Mullene]	To explore the dynamics of receiving verbal and nonverbal communication cues that are in conflict with one another. To examine how nonverbal cues can convey listener attitudes that can affect the communication process. To develop an understanding of the importance and impact of being direct and congruent in all forms of interpersonal communication	Approximately forty-five minutes to one hour	VII-34
307	**Maze:** One-Way and Two-Way Communication [G.L. Talbot]	To experience the effects of free versus restricted communication in accomplishing a task. To explore the impact of communication processes on the development of trust between a leader and a follower	Approximately one and one-half to two hours	VIII-64
309	**Resistance:** A Role Play [H.B. Karp]	To provide an opportunity to experience the effects of two different approaches to dealing with resistance. To increase awareness of typical responses to attempts to break down resistance. To develop strategies for coping with resistance from others	Two to two and one-half hours	VIII-75

Communication Awareness Experiments (Oral) (Continued)

Number	Title [Author]	Goals	Time Required	Volume & Page No.
310	**Organizational TA:** Interpersonal Communication [R. Strand & F.R. Wickert]	To gain insight into the effects on communication of the three ego states: parent (P), adult (A), and child (C). To have the experience of operating from each of these three ego stages in confrontation situations. To acquire skills in observing interactions based on these three ego states. To explore the benefits of operating from an adult ego state in confrontation situations	Approximately two hours	VIII-83

Communication Awareness Experiments (Nonverbal)

Number	Title [Author]	Goals	Time Required	Volume & Page No.
22	**Nonverbal Communication: A Collection of Activities**	To learn new ways of expressing one's feelings, independent of one's vocabulary. To express feelings authentically using nonverbal symbolism. To focus on nonverbal cues that one emits	Varies with each activity	I-101
44	**Nonverbal Communication: A Collection**	To learn new ways of expressing one's feelings, independent of one's vocabulary. To express feelings authentically using nonverbal symbolism. To focus on nonverbal cues that one emits	Varies with each activity	II-94

Communication Awareness Experiments (Nonverbal) (Continued)

Number	Title [Author]	Goals	Time Required	Volume & Page No.
50	**Behavior Description Triads:** Reading Body Language	To practice describing nonverbal behavior objectively, without interpretation. To study the body-language messages that accompany verbalization. To alert group members to the variety of signals they use to communicate	Approximately fifteen minutes	III-6
72	**Nonverbal Communication:** A Collection	To learn new ways of expressing one's feelings, independent of one's vocabulary. To express feelings authentically using nonverbal symbolism. To focus on nonverbal cues that one emits	Varies with each activity	III-97
286	**Gestures:** Perceptions and Responses [S.L. Norman]	To provide an opportunity for participants to examine the perceptual biases operating in their interpretations of gestures. To increase awareness of the ambiguity inherent in various forms of nonverbal communication. To demonstrate how one gesture can elicit different feeling responses among different persons. To examine the principle that verbal and nonverbal communication must be congruent to be effective	Approximately one and one-half hours	'81-28

Communication Awareness Experiments (Oral/Nonverbal)

Number	Title [Author]	Goals	Time Required	Volume & Page No.
153	**Babel:** Interpersonal Communication [P.M. Ericson]	To examine language barriers which contribute to breakdowns in communication. To demonstrate the anxieties and frustrations that may be felt when communicating under difficult circumstances. To illustrate the impact of nonverbal communication when verbal communication is ineffective and/or restricted	Approximately two hours	V-16
175	**Blindfolds:** A Dyadic Experience [J.I. Costigan & A.L. Dirks]	To demonstrate and experience the need for visual cues in perception and communication. To demonstrate the need for visual cues in the definition of "personal space"	Approximately one hour	'76-13

Developing Interpersonal Trust in Dyads

Number	Title [Author]	Goals	Time Required	Volume & Page No.
21	**Dyadic Encounter:** A Program for Developing Relationships [J.E. Jones & J.J. Jones]	To explore knowing and trusting another person through mutual self-disclosure and risk taking	A minimum of two hours	I-90
70	**Intimacy Program:** Developing Personal Relationships [*adapted from S.M. Jourard*]	To accelerate the getting-acquainted process in groups. To study the experience of self-disclosure. To develop authenticity in groups	Approximately one and one-half hours	III-89

Developing Interpersonal Trust in Dyads (Continued)

Number	Title [Author]	Goals	Time Required	Volume & Page No.
116	**Dialog:** A Program for Developing Work Relationships [J.E. Jones & J.J. Jones]	To increase openness in work relationships. To generate higher trust in interpersonal relations in work settings. To clarify assumptions that persons who work together make about each other and each other's jobs	A minimum of two hours	IV-66
138	**Party Conversations:** A FIRO Role-Play [C.L. Kormanski]	To experiment with different types of interpersonal behavior. To demonstrate the concepts in Schutz's theory of interpersonal relations	Approximately two and one-half hours	'75-10
169	**Dyadic Renewal:** A Program for Developing Ongoing Relationships [C.A. Kelley & J.S. Colladay]	To periodically explore various aspects of a relationship through mutual self-disclosure and risk taking	A minimum of two hours	V-116
180	**Disclosing and Predicting:** A Perception-Checking Activity [J. Lalanne]	To aid participants in developing social perception skills. To familiarize participants with the concept of accurate empathy. To demonstrate the effects that first impressions can have on perception	Approximately thirty minutes	'76-46
190	**Letter Exchange:** A Dyadic Focus on Feelings [A.G. Kirn]	To provide a practical, low-threat, repeatable framework for sharing feelings as a step toward building a dyadic relationship. To promote self-disclosure and interpersonal risk taking	Approximately one hour	'77-28

Developing Interpersonal Trust in Dyads (Continued)

Number	Title [Author]	Goals	Time Required	Volume & Page No.
220	**Dyadic Risk Taking:** A Perception Check [K.G. Albrecht & W.C. Boshear]	To experience the feelings associated with mild risk-taking behavior. To experiment with controlling the level of risk one is willing to take. To experience specific feedback on the degree to which another perceives one's risk	Approximately one hour	VI-130
242	**Conflict Management:** Dyadic Sharing [M. Robert]	To identify and share reactions to ways of dealing with conflict. To explore new ideas about managing conflict	Approximately one hour	'79-54
262	**Physical Characteristics: Dyadic Perception Checking** [A.J. Schuh]	To examine one's reactions to the physical characteristics of others. To learn to observe others more accurately. To study the effects of generalizing and stereotyping	Forty-five minutes to one hour	VII-108

Sexual Awareness

Number	Title [Author]	Goals	Time Required	Volume & Page No.
226	**Sexual Assessment:** Self-Disclosure [P.S. Weikert]	To share sexual perceptions, feelings, attitudes, values, behaviors, and expectations. To clarify one's sexuality through self-disclosure. To gain insight into the sexual dimensions of other persons	Approximately two and one-half hours	'78-36
249	**Sexual Values:** Relationship Clarification [P.S. Weikert]	To identify one's own values about a sexual relationship. To become aware of the sexual values of others. To increase awareness of the many components of sexual relationships	One and one-half hours	VII-24

Sexual Awareness (Continued)

Number	Title [Author]	Goals	Time Required	Volume & Page No.
272	Sexual Attraction: A Written Role Play [J.B. Driscoll & R.A. Bova]	To explore the dynamics of sexual attraction among co-workers. To heighten awareness of the effect that assumptions can have on the shaping of an evolving relationship. To provide an opportunity for participants to explore their personal interpretations of, assumptions about, and responses to issues regarding sexual attraction	Approximately one hour and forty-five minutes	'80-26

Listening

Number	Title [Author]	Goals	Time Required	Volume & Page No.
8	Listening Triads: Building Communications Skills	To develop skills in active listening. To study barriers to effective listening	Approximately forty-five minutes	I-31
52	Not-Listening: A Dyadic Role-Play [H.B. Karp]	To allow participants to experience the frustration of not being heard. To promote listening readiness	Approximately thirty minutes	III-10
152	Helping Relationships: Verbal and Nonverbal Communication [C.G. Carney]	To demonstrate the effects of posturing and eye contact on helping relationships. To focus group members' attention on the impact of their nonverbal behaviors on other individuals. To teach basic nonverbal listening and attending skills	Approximately thirty minutes	V-13

Listening (Continued)

Number	Title [Author]	Goals	Time Required	Volume & Page No.
238	**Defensive and Supportive Communication:** A Dyadic Role Play [G.W. Combs]	To examine the dynamics of defensive and supportive communication in supervisor/subordinate relationships. To develop skills in listening to and understanding a contrasting point of view. To explore the concept of synergy in dyadic communication. To examine the expectations that defensive communication creates for a continuing relationship	Approximately one and one-half hours	'79-28
252	**Active Listening:** A Communication-Skills Practice [J.N. Wismer]	To identify the emotional messages that are often hidden in communication. To gain practice in active-listening skills	Approximately one and one-half hours	VII-39
257	**Sunglow:** An Appraisal Role Play [J.M. Rigby]	To practice skills in counseling, coaching, and active listening. To increase awareness of behavioral and interpersonal factors that influence an interview. To provide feedback on interviewing effectiveness	Two to two and one-half hours	VII-73

Interviewing

Number	Title [Author]	Goals	Time Required	Volume & Page No.
142	**Live Case:** A Group Diagnosis [R.K. Conyne & D.H. Frey]	To illustrate problems involved in overgeneralizing. To practice interviewing techniques as a method of generating data about an individual. To study the process of forming hypotheses from available information	Approximately two hours	'75-40

Assertion

Number	Title [Author]	Goals	Time Required	Volume & Page No.
130	**Conflict Fantasy:** A Self-Examination [J.A. Stepsis]	To facilitate awareness of strategies for dealing with conflict situations. To examine methods of responding to conflict. To introduce the strategy of negotiation and to present the skills required for successful negotiation	Approximately forty-five minutes	'74-22
181	**Boasting:** A Self-Enhancement Activity [J.J. Rosenblum & J.E. Jones]	To help participants identify, own, and share their personal strengths. To explore feelings and reactions to sharing "boasts" with other participants. To experience the enhanced sense of personal power in announcing one's strengths to others	Approximately one hour and fifteen minutes	'76-49
206	**Submission/Aggression/ Assertion:** Nonverbal Components [G.N. Weiskott & M.E. Sparks]	To experience and differentiate the nonverbal components of assertive behavior from those of aggressive and submissive (non-assertive) behavior. To increase awareness of one's own assertive behavior	Approximately thirty minutes to one hour	VI-36
219	**Escalation:** An Assertion Activity [C. Kelley]	To allow participants to experience success in communicating while under stress. To enable participants to practice communicating effectively in stressful situations	One to two hours	VI-127
306	**Praise:** Giving and Receiving Positive Feedback [T.J. Mason]	To develop an awareness of one's own accomplishments. To practice giving public recognition to others. To become aware of one's responses to recognition from others	One an one-half to two hours	VIII-61

GROUP CHARACTERISTICS
Process Observation/Awareness

Number	Title [Author]	Goals	Time Required	Volume & Page No.
6	**Group-On-Group:** A Feedback Experience	To develop skills in process observation. To develop skills in giving appropriate feedback to individual group members	Approximately one hour	I-22
9	**Committee Meeting:** Demonstrating Hidden Agendas [*based on J. Gold & L. Miller*]	To illustrate the effects of hidden agendas on task accomplishment in a work group	Approximately one and one-half hours	I-36
10	**Process Observation:** A Guide	To provide feedback to a group concerning its process. To provide experience for group members in observing process variables in group meetings	Minimum of ten minutes for processing	I-45
29	**Group Tasks:** A Collection of Activities	To be used in studying group process	Varies with each activity	II-16
37	**Self-Interaction-Task:** Process Observation Guides [J.E. Jones]	To practice observing small-group process. To gain experience in reporting process observations to a group. To provide instrumented feedback on one's interpersonal orientations	Two hours	II-68
39	**Group Development:** A Graphic Analysis [J.E. Jones]	To compare the development of a small group along the dimensions of task functions and personal relations. To compare members' perceptions of the developmental status of a group at a given time	Approximately forty-five minutes	II-76

Process Observation/Awareness (Continued)

Number	Title [Author]	Goals	Time Required	Volume & Page No.
79	**What to Look For in Groups:** An Observation Guide [P.G. Hanson]	To assist group members in understanding and being more perceptive about group process	Three hours	'72-19
124	**The In-Group:** Dynamics of Exclusion [G. Goldberg]	To allow participants to experience consciously excluding and being excluded. To confront feelings which exlusion generates. To examine processes by which social identity is conferred by the excluding group and accepted by the excluded member	Approximately one and one-half hours	IV-112
126	**Cog's Ladder:** A Process-Observation Activity [G.O. Charrier]	To enhance awareness of factors which distinguish process from content in group interaction. To explore a model of group development	One hour	'74-8
208	**Team Development:** A TORI Model [G.R. Gemmill]	To study TORI growth processes. To practice applying a theoretical model to group self-diagnosis	Approximately two and one-half hours	VI-54
254	**Stones, Bands, and Circle:** Sociogram Activities [D.E. Miskiman; J.E. Hoover & M.A. Goldstein; D. Anderson]	To explore existing levels of interaction, influence, and inclusion in a group. To develop an awareness of group dynamics	Approximately forty-five minutes to one hour per activity	VII-53
270	**Baseball Game:** Group Membership Functions [R.W. Rasberry]	To gain insight into how one is perceived by others. To study the variety of functions performed by group members. To introduce a novel way of characterizing group-member roles	Approximately three hours	'80-14

Process Observation/Awareness (Continued)

Number	Title [Author]	Goals	Time Required	Volume & Page No.
276	**Slogans:** A Group-Development Activity [S.M. Sant]	To experience the processes and feelings that arise when a new member joins an ongoing group with defined tasks and roles. To explore the coping mechanisms adopted by the individual and the group to deal with entry problems. To examine functional and dysfunctional coping strategies of groups	Approximately three hours	'80-51
299	**Group Identity:** A Developmental Planning Session [K.W. Howard]	To provide the members of an intact group with a model for understanding the factors that influence its development. To enable the members of an intact group to identify its current stage of growth. To promote group cohesiveness by exploring the needs and interests of its members	Approximately two hours	VIII-25

Leadership-Membership/Power

Number	Title [Author]	Goals	Time Required	Volume & Page No.
59	**Line-Up and Power: Inversion:** An Experiment	To expand the individual's awareness of his influence on the group. To experience power inversion	Approximately one and one-half hours	III-46
121	**Toothpicks:** An Analysis of Helping Behaviors [R.R. Middleman]	To identify differing approaches to assisting others in a task. To explore the effects of the various helping approaches on task accomplishment and interpersonal relations	Approximately one hour	IV-99

Leadership-Membership/Power (Continued)

Number	Title [Author]	Goals	Time Required	Volume & Page No.
167	**Cups:** A Power Experience [A.J. Reilly]	To increase awareness of the meanings of power. To experience giving, receiving, and not receiving power	Approximately two hours	V-111
266	**Power Personalities:** An OD Role Play [L.A. Jean, J.R. Pilgrim, G.N. Powell, D.K. Stoltz, & O.S. White]	To provide an opportunity to practice various power styles and behaviors. To learn which power-seeking tactics and bases of power are effective or ineffective in a problem-solving situation. To examine individual perceptions of and reactions to various power strategies	Approximately one and one-half to two hours	VII-127
277	**Power and Affiliation:** A Role Play [J.F. Veiga & J.N. Yanouzas]	To become better acquainted with positive and negative aspects of power and affiliation. To explore the dynamics of power and affiliation in managerial situations	Approximately one hour and forty-five minutes	'80-54

Leadership-Membership/Styles

Number	Title [Author]	Goals	Time Required	Volume & Page No.
3	**T-P Leadership Questionnaire:** An Assessment of Style [*adapted from Sergiovanni, Metzcus, & Burden*]	To evaluate oneself in terms of task orientation and people orientation	Approximately forty-five minutes	I-7
154	**Styles of Leadership:** A Series of Role Plays [G.M. Phillips]	To explore the impact that leaders have on decision making in groups. To demonstrate the effects of hidden agendas	Approximately two hours	V-19

Leadership-Membership/Styles (Continued)

Number	Title [Author]	Goals	Time Required	Volume & Page No.
162	**Pins and Straws:** Leadership Styles [H.L. Fromkin]	To dramatize three general styles of leadership: autocratic, laissez-faire, and democratic. To increase awareness of how different styles of leadership can affect the performance of subordinates. To study the phenomenon of competition among groups	Approximately two hours	V-78
207	**Staff Meeting:** A Leadership Role Play [E.M. Schuttenberg]	To illustrate various styles of leadership and patterns of accommodation. To explore the effects of the interaction of leadership style and pattern of accommodation on individual motivation and decision making	Approximately two and one-half hours. Additional time is required if lecturettes are to be presented	VI-39
274	**Choosing an Apartment:** Authority Issues in Groups [J.J. Szucko, R.L. Greenblatt, & C.B. Keys]	To experience the impact of authoritarian behavior during a competitive activity. To increase personal awareness of reactions to authoritarian behavior. To experience the effects of hidden agendas on decision-making processes	Two hours	'80-37
296	**Boss Wanted:** Identifying Leadership Characteristics [G.L. Williams]	To allow individuals to examine their personal criteria for a good manager. To compare preferences about managerial qualities. To increase awareness of one's own current managerial strengths and weaknesses	Approximately one and one-half hours	VIII-15

Leadership-Membership/Motivation

Number	Title [Author]	Goals	Time Required	Volume & Page No.
60	**Dividing the Loot:** Symbolic Feedback	To provide symbolic feedback to participants. To explore the responsibilities and problems of leadership	One hour	III-49
100	**Motivation:** A Feedback Exercise [D.F. Michalak]	To learn the concepts in Maslow's Need Hierarchy. To get feedback on one's use of motivational techniques in terms of Maslow's Need Hierarchy	At least one-half hour	'73-43
159	**Fork-Labyrinth:** Leadership Practice [J.F. Veiga]	To diagnose the behavior of leaders and followers in a small group performing a complex competitive task. To teach "on-line" feedback and coaching on leadership behavior. To practice different leadership behaviors	Approximately three hours	V-53
204	**Motivation:** A Supervisory-Skill Activity [K. Frey & J.D. Jackson]	To demonstrate the value of goal setting for task achievement. To demonstrate the positive role of a supervisor in developing the motivation to achieve	Approximately one hour	VI-28
253	**Penny Pitch:** Demonstrating Reinforcement Styles [B.F. Spencer]	To demonstrate how positive or negative reinforcement can affect motivation and task accomplishment. To increase awareness of responses to interventions made by persons with position and status	Approximately one hour	VII-46

Leadership-Membership/Effect on Groups

Number	Title [Author]	Goals	Time Required	Volume & Page No.
35	**Auction:** An Intergroup Competition [J.W. Pfeiffer]	To explore relationships between leadership and decision making in a competitive situation. To illustrate effects of task success or failure on the selection of group representatives and leaders	Approximately one hour	II-58
41	**Status-Interaction Study:** A Multiple-Role-Play [J.W. Pfeiffer]	To explore effects of status differences and deference on interaction among group members	Forty-five minutes	II-85
192	**Package Tour:** Leadership and Consensus Seeking [P. Mumford]	To demonstrate the need for consensus on group goals. To demonstrate leadership techniques and strategies in conducting meetings. To experience the impact of hidden agendas on group decision making	Approximately two hours	'77-35
195	**Executive Pie:** A Power Experience [S.H. Putnam]	To enhance the awareness of the uses of power in group decision making. To explore the values inherent in various styles of leadership. To simulate a common organizational problem	Approximately one hour	'77-54
239	**Race from Outer Space:** An Awareness Activity [D.G. Cash]	To compare qualities and skills needed to lead a single racial group and those needed to lead a mixed racial group. To increase awareness of social values and how these may differ among people and groups	One and one-half to two hours	'79-38
288	**Project Colossus:** Intergroup Competition [J.V. Fee]	To explore the dynamics of status, power, and special knowledge in decision making. To examine the effects of intragroup competition on team functioning	One to one and one-half hours	'81-43

Leadership-Membership/Effect on Groups (Continued)

Number	Title [Author]	Goals	Time Required	Volume & Page No.
290	Dynasell: Hidden Agendas and Trust [W.W. Kibler]	To demonstrate the impact of distrust on collaboration in a task group. To heighten awareness of one's personal responses when the motives of others are in question	One and one-half to two hours	'81-50

Communication

Number	Title [Author]	Goals	Time Required	Volume & Page No.
110	Organization Structures: Communication Patterns [T. Irwin]	To demonstrate the varying effectiveness of different organization structures. To diagnose working relationships within an intact group. To illustrate less efficient modes of communication. To illustrate perceived alienation	Approximately one hour	IV-34
139	Faculty Meeting: A Multiple Role-Play [F.H. McCarty & B. Nisenholz]	To study behaviors that facilitate and that block communication in groups. To explore the effects of process feedback on team functioning	Approximately two and one-half hours	'75-15

Values Clarification/Stereotyping

Number	Title [Author]	Goals	Time Required	Volume & Page No.
62	Polarization: A Demonstration [J.E. Jones & J.J. Jones]	To explore the experience of interpersonal polarization—its forms and effects. To study conflict management and resolution	Approximately two hours	III-57
63	Discrimination: Simulation Activities	To simulate the experience of discrimination. To study phenomena of stereotyping people	Varies with each activity	III-62

Values Clarification/Stereotyping (Continued)

Number	Title [Author]	Goals	Time Required	Volume & Page No.
94	**Traditional American Values:** Intergroup Confrontation	To clarify one's own value system. To explore values held in common within a group. To study differences existing between groups. To begin to remove stereotypes held by members of different groups	Approximately one and one-half hours	'73-23
95	**Sex-Role Stereotyping** [M. Carson]	To make distinctions between thoughts and feelings about sex-role stereotyping. To examine one's own reactions to sexism in a mixed group. To link feeling feedback to observable behavior. To avoid over-generalization. To explore the experience of interpersonal polarization—its forms and effects. To study conflict resolution	Approximately two hours	'73-26
113	**Growth Group Values:** A Clarification Exercise [O. Elliott & D. Zellinger]	To clarify one's own value system. To explore values held in common within a group. To study differences existing between groups. To begin to remove stereotypes held by members of different groups	Approximately one and one-half hours	IV-45
127	**Leadership Characteristics:** Examining Values in Personnel Selection [C.L. Kormanski]	To compare the results of individual decision making and group decision making. To explore values underlying leadership characteristics. To examine effects of value judgments on personnel selection	Approximately two hours	'74-13

Values Clarification/Stereotyping (Continued)

Number	Title [Author]	Goals	Time Required	Volume & Page No.
135	Kidney Machine: Group Decision-Making [G.M. Phillips]	To explore choices involving values. To study problem-solving procedures in groups. To examine the impact of individuals' values and attitudes on group decision making	Approximately one hour	'74-78
184	Sex-Role Attributes: A Collection of Activities	To expand personal awareness. To explore the cultural biases and prejudices that the sexes have regarding each other	Varies with each activity	'76-63
203	Headbands: Group Role Expectations [E. Sieburg]	To experience the pressures of role expectations. To demonstrate the effects of role expectations on individual behavior in a group. To explore the effects of role pressures on total group performance	Approximately forty-five minutes	VI-25
215	Who Gets Hired?: A Male/Female Role Play [L.V. Entrekin & G.N. Soutar]	To clarify one's personal values regarding sex discrimination. To examine the values held in common on this subject within a group. To explore whether groups of different sexual composition have differences in such values. To study the way in which such issues are resolved within a group. To gain insight into the subtle aspects of discrimination	One to one and one-half hours	VI-106
235	Who Killed John Doe?: A Value-Clarification Activity [C.A. Hart]	To articulate individual opinions about social and individual responsibilities. To explore and clarify personal values. To participate in shared decision making	Approximately one hour	'79-15

Values Clarification/Stereotyping (Continued)

Number	Title [Author]	Goals	Time Required	Volume & Page No.
248	**Alpha II:** Clarifying Sexual Values [D. Keyworth]	To explore attitudes regarding sexual mores. To compare sexual values with others. To practice group consensus seeking	Two to two and one-half hours	VII-19
258	**Sex-Role Attitudes:** Personal Feedback [B.P. Holleran]	To develop an understanding of the ways in which sex-based attitudes influence and are inferred from communication. To discuss attitudes and prejudices about sexes in a nonthreatening environment. To increase awareness of and provide feedback on one's own attitudes, beliefs, and behaviors in regard to sex differences	Approximately two to three hours	VII-85

GROUP TASK BEHAVIOR
Problem Solving/Awareness

Number	Title [Author]	Goals	Time Required	Volume & Page No.
7	**Broken Squares:** Nonverbal Problem-Solving	To analyze some aspects of cooperation in solving a group problem. To sensitize participants to behaviors which may contribute toward or obstruct the solving of a group problem	Approximately forty-five minutes	I-25
102	**Shoe Store:** Group Problem-Solving [A.M. Zelmer]	To observe communication patterns in group problem solving. To explore interpersonal influence in problem solving	Thirty to sixty minutes	IV-5

Problem Solving/Awareness (Continued)

Number	Title [Author]	Goals	Time Required	Volume & Page No.
103	**Joe Doodlebug:** Group Problem-Solving [*adapted from* M. Rokeach]	To explore the effect of participants' response sets in a group problem-solving activity. To observe leadership behavior in a problem-solving situation	Approximately forty-five minutes	IV-8
111	**System Problems:** A Diagnostic Activity [M.S. Perlmutter & C.R. Ahrons]	To generate data about the functioning of an intact group or a growth group. To diagnose the way a system approaches problem solving	Approximately one hour	IV-38
134	**Hung Jury:** A Decision-Making Simulation [S.C. Iman, B.D. Jones, & A.S. Crown]	To study decision-making processes	Approximately two hours	'74-64
200	**Word-Letter:** A Problem-Solving Activity [J.P. Berliner]	To demonstrate how problems are resolved when the alternatives are not clearly defined or the situation is ambiguous. To explore group problem-solving processes	Approximately one and one-half hours	VI-15
221	**Numbers:** A Problem-Solving Activity [B.D. Ruben & R.W. Budd]	To demonstrate how new information and assistance can improve performance. To discover how experience facilitates task accomplishment	One to one and one-half hours	'78-9
240	**Puzzle Cards:** Approaches to Problem Solving [E.J. Cummins]	To generate an interest in and understanding of different approaches to problem solving. To compare advantages and disadvantages of different problem-solving methods	One to one and one-half hours	'79-41

Problem Solving/Awareness (Continued)

Number	Title [Author]	Goals	Time Required	Volume & Page No.
260	Island Commission: Group Problem Solving [P.G. Gillan]	To experience the issues involved in long-range social planning. To study emergent group dynamics and leadership in the completion of a group task. To explore aspects of communication, problem solving, and decision making in a work group	Two to two and one-half hours	VII-99
285	Analytical or Creative?: A Problem-Solving Comparison [B.A. McDonald]	To provide an opportunity to compare analytical and creative problem-solving approaches. To increase awareness of one's own capabilities in and preferences for these two approaches to problem solving	Approximately one and one-half hours	'81-24
287	Four-Letter Words: Examining Task-Group Processes [W.J. Cox]	To study the behavior of an unstructured group in accomplishing a complex task. To heighten awareness of the importance of correct interpretation of written task instructions. To enable group members to compare observed behavior with typical task-group behavior. To assist group members to better perceive and understand individual interactions within a task group	Approximately two and one-half hours	'81-34
312	Vacation Schedule: Group Problem Solving [L.B. Day & M. Blizzard]	To explore the advantages and disadvantages of using group-decision-making procedures to resolve complex issues. To increase awareness of supervisory responsibilities in decision-making situations	Approximately two hours	VIII-100

Problem Solving/Awareness (Continued)

Number	Title [Author]	Goals	Time Required	Volume & Page No.
313	Tangram: Leadership Dimensions [E. Casais]	To identify key functions of a task-team leader. To examine the process of leading a team toward the accomplishment of a task. To experience the information-sharing process within a task team. To provide an opportunity to observe the effects of communication processes on members of a task team	Approximately two hours	VIII-108

Generating Alternatives

Number	Title [Author]	Goals	Time Required	Volume & Page No.
53	Brainstorming: A Problem-Solving Activity	To generate an extensive number of ideas or solutions to a problem by suspending criticism and evaluation. To develop skills in creative problem solving	Approximately one hour	III-14
76	Quaker Meeting	To generate a large number of ideas, suggestions, approaches to a problem or topic when the group is too large to employ brainstorming techniques. To gather data quickly for a large group to process	Fifteen minutes for the actual "Quaker meeting" plus processing time appropriate for the particular group	'72-11

Generating Alternatives (Continued)

Number	Title [Author]	Goals	Time Required	Volume & Page No.
141	**Nominal Group Technique:** An Applied Group Problem-Solving Activity [D.L. Ford, Jr.; *adapted from* A. Delbecq & A. Van de Ven]	To increase creativity and participation in group meetings involving problem-solving and/or fact-finding tasks. To develop or expand perception of critical issues within problem areas. To identify priorities of selected issues within problems, considering the viewpoints of differently oriented groups	Two hours	'75-35
185	**Poems:** Interpersonal Communication [B.P. Holleran]	To experience the interaction conditions necessary for creative problem solving. To arrive at a creative solution in a group situation	One to one and one-half hours	'77-13

Group Feedback

Number	Title [Author]	Goals	Time Required	Volume & Page No.
17	**Leveling:** Giving and Receiving Adverse Feedback [J.W. Pfeiffer]	To let participants compare their perceptions of how a group sees them with the actual feedback obtained from the group. To legitimize giving negative feedback within a group. To develop skills in giving negative feedback	Approximately ten minutes per participant	I-79
18	**Dependency-Intimacy:** A Feedback Experience [J.E. Jones]	To provide instrumented feedback. To study how the personal dimensions of dependency and intimacy affect group development	Approximately one and one-half hours	I-82

Group Feedback (Continued)

Number	Title [Author]	Goals	Time Required	Volume & Page No.
38	**Role Nominations:** A Feedback Experience [*based on* K.D. Benne & P. Sheats]	To provide feedback to group members on the roles fellow members see them playing. To study various types of roles in relation to group goals. To demonstrate that leadership in a small group consists of several functions which should be shared among members	Approximately one and one-half hours	II-72
57	**Nominations: Personal Instrumented Feedback**	To provide feedback to group members on how they are perceived by each other. To analyze the climate and the norms of the group by studying members' behavior, composition of the group, and members' expectations of each other	Approximately one hour	III-33
66	**Team-Building:** A Feedback Experience	To help an intact work group diagnose its functioning. To establish a co-operative expectation within a task group. To assist a "real life" group or business manager (leader, chairman, supervisor) to develop norms of openness, trust, and interdependence among team members and/or members of his organization	A minimum of one day	III-73
84	**Psychomat**	To provide an atmosphere in which participants can encounter each other in a variety of ways. To encourage creative, sensitive risk taking on the part of participants. To explore reactions to a highly unstructured interpersonal situation	Six to nine hours	'72-58

Group Feedback (Continued)

Number	Title [Author]	Goals	Time Required	Volume & Page No.
104	**The Gift of Happiness:** Experiencing Positive Feedback [D. Keyworth]	To promote a climate of trust, self-worth, and positive reinforcement within a small group. To experience giving and receiving positive feedback in a nonthreatening way	Approximately five minutes per participant and about thirty minutes for processing	IV-15
118	**Twenty-Five Questions:** A Team Development Exercise [J.E. Jones]	To enhance work relationships in intact groups. To stimulate group discussion about work-related topics. To clarify assumptions that team members make about each other	Approximately one and one-half hours	IV-88
291	**I Hear that You . . . :** Giving and Receiving Feedback [D.P. Danko & R. Cherry]	To establish a climate conducive to giving and receiving feedback in established work groups. To practice active listening and feedback skills. To help make work-group behavior more understandable by linking behavior to perceptions. To improve work-group relations and climate	One and one-half to two hours	'81-54
316	**Group Sociogram:** Intragroup Communication [T.J. Mallinson]	To identify existing patterns of interaction and influence in an intact group. To increase awareness of the effects of group dynamics on intragroup communication patterns	Approximately one and one-half hours	VIII-131

Competition (Win-Lose)

Number	Title [Author]	Goals	Time Required	Volume & Page No.
32	Model-Building: An Intergroup Competition	To study interpersonal and intergroup competition phenomena. To explore the feeling content and behavioral results of winning and losing. To provide feedback to group members on their contributions in a task situation	Approximately one and one-half hours	II-29
54	Towers: An Intergroup Competition	To study phenomena of competition among groups. To explore the feeling content and behavioral outcomes of winning and losing. To provide a basis for feedback to group members on their relations with other group members and their productivity in a task situation	Approximately one and one-half hours	III-17
81	Intergroup Model-Building: The Lego Man [W.B. Reddy & O. Kroeger]	To extract the learnings from a competitive team-work experience, in terms of leadership style, developing alternatives, dominance and submission within teams, and distribution of work and resources. To diagnose the dynamics of an intact group in terms of role taking	Approximately two hours	'72-36
105	Wooden Blocks: A Competition Exercise [A.M. Zelmer]	To explore individual and small group goal-setting behavior and achievement motivation. To study interpersonal and intergroup competition phenomena. To explore feelings and outcomes of winning and losing	Approximately one hour	IV-18

Competition (Win-Lose) (Continued)

Number	Title [Author]	Goals	Time Required	Volume & Page No.
150	**Riddles:** Intergroup Competition [B.P. Holleran]	To observe competitive behavior among groups. To determine how a group interacts with other groups when it is dependent on them for the completion of its task	Approximately one and one-half hours	V-5
161	**Lego Bridge:** Intergroup Competition [P. Mumford]	To observe spontaneous patterns of organization in work groups. To explore the relationship between planning and production. To study the effects of intergroup competition on team functioning	Approximately one and one-half hours	V-73
210	**Darts:** Competition and Motivation [S. Dolinsky]	To develop awareness of the factors involved in motivation. To increase awareness of the effects of motivation/incentives on the attitudes and performance of a given task in an intergroup competitive situation	Approximately one and one-half hours	VI-61
218	**Spy:** An Intergroup Activity [S.J. Schoen]	To explore the impact of competition between groups. To demonstrate different methods of group problem solving. To examine the dynamics of suspicion and distrust in a group. To observe the process of a leader-less group in the completion of a specific task	Approximately one and one-half hours	VI-117
256	**Slingshots:** Studying Group Dynamics [K.M. Bond]	To experience the group dynamics involved in task accomplishment. To study the effects of competition on group functioning. To experience the functional and dysfunctional aspects of process interventions	Approximately one hour and fifteen minutes	VII-69

Competition (Win-Lose) (Continued)

Number	Title [Author]	Goals	Time Required	Volume & Page No.
308	**Structures:** Intergroup Competition [A.C. Stein, S.C. Iman, & A.A. Ramos]	To study the effects of intergroup competition on group processes. To identify helps and hindrances to task accomplishment. To demonstrate the impact of effective and ineffective communication processes in task groups	Approximately two hours	VIII-69
311	**Risk Game:** Competition and Team Building	To increase awareness of one's preferred level of risk taking. To increase awareness of how the attitudes of others can affect one's choices and level of risk taking. To study the effects of intergroup competition on intragroup communication processes	Approximately two hours	VIII-93

Competition and Collaboration (Win-Lose/Win-Win)

Number	Title [Author]	Goals	Time Required	Volume & Page No.
36	**Win As Much As You Can:** An Intergroup Competition [*based on* W. Gellerman]	To dramatize the merits of both competitive and collaborative models within the context of intragroup and intergroup relations. To illustrate the impact of win-lose situations	Approximately one hour	II-62
61	**Prisoners' Dilemma:** An Intergroup Competition	To explore trust between group members and effects of betrayal of trust. To demonstrate effects of interpersonal competition. To dramatize the merit of a collaborative posture in intragroup and intergroup relations	Approximately one hour	III-52

Competition and Collaboration (Win-Lose/Win-Win) (Continued)

Number	Title [Author]	Goals	Time Required	Volume & Page No.
78	**Unequal Resources**	To provide an opportunity for observing group use of resources which have been distributed un-equally. To observe bargaining processes	Approximately one hour	'72-17
83	**Decisions:** An Intergroup Negotiation [H.I. Feir, with R.J. Turner, R. Cox, D.N. Kanouse, & R.G. Mason]	To experience the issues surrounding intergroup trust building and trust betrayal. To explore considerations of inter-group competition versus collaboration. To examine limited communication under stress. To study negotiation and negotia-tion strategies. To con-sider group decision-making processes	A minimum of four and one-half hours	'72-51
147	**World Bank:** An Intergroup Negotiation [N.H. Berkowitz & H.A. Hornstein]	To experience the conflict between advantages of cooperation and advan-tages of competition in a mixed-motive dilemma. To explore some dynamics of trust between groups. To practice negotiation skills	Approximately three hours	'75-56
164	**Testing:** Intergroup Competition [P.R. Scholtes]	To explore the impact of the lack of communica-tion in competitive situa-tions. To demonstrate the need for collaboration and interdependence	Approximately one and one-half hours	V-91
165	**Marbles: A Community Experiment** [*adapted from* F.L. Goodman]	To study community from the perspectives of establishing, enforcing, and interpreting rules. To explore rule-governed behaviors	Approximately two hours	V-98

Competition and Collaboration (Win-Lose/Win-Win) (Continued)

Number	Title [Author]	Goals	Time Required	Volume & Page No.
178	**Al Kohbari:** An Information-Sharing Multiple Role Play [R.E. Mattingly]	To study how information relevant to a task is shared within work groups. To observe problem-solving strategies within work groups. To explore the effects of collaboration and competition in group problem solving. To demonstrate the effects of hidden agendas on group decision making	Approximately two hours	'76-26
179	X-Y: A Three-Way Intergroup Competition [G.J. Rath, J. Kisch, & H.E. Miller]	To explore interpersonal trust. To demonstrate the effects of cooperation, competition, and betrayal. To dramatize the advantages of both competitive and collaborative models in intergroup relations	Approximately two hours	'76-41
189	**Blue/Green:** An Intergroup Negotiation [*adapted from* J. Owens]	To explore the element of trust between group members and the effects of the betrayal of trust. To demonstrate the effects of competition and collaboration in intergroup relationships. To study the effects of win-lose, win-win, and lose-lose strategies in negotiations between groups	One and one-half hours	'77-24
205	**Circle in the Square:** A Cooperation/ Competition Activity [C.E. Lee]	To demonstrate how cooperation and competition can affect winning and losing. To explore how winning and losing are defined, perceived, and measured	Approximately one hour	VI-32

Competition and Collaboration (Win-Lose/Win-Win) (Continued)

Number	Title [Author]	Goals	Time Required	Volume & Page No.
212	**Murder One:** Information Sharing [D.K. McLeod]	To explore the effects of cooperation-collaboration versus competition in group problem solving. To demonstrate the need for information sharing and other problem-solving strategies in a task-oriented group. To study the roles that emerge in a task group	One and one-half hours	VI-75
231	**Balance of Power:** A Cooperation/ Competition Activity [L. Parshall]	To explore the effects of collaboration and competition strategies in group problem solving. To study how task-relevant information is shared between groups. To increase awareness of the influence that leaders (or political systems) have on decision making in groups	Approximately two and one-half hours	'78-63
237	**Line of Four:** An Intergroup Competition [W.R. Mulford]	To examine a group's communication, planning, and collaborative behavior. To examine the use of self-imposed rules of behavior. To explore the dynamics of intergroup competition	Approximately one and one-half hours	'79-21
243	**Paper Box:** An Intergroup-Competition Activity [J.G. Clawson]	To study intra- and intergroup relations and conflict. To demonstrate the effects of collaboration versus those of competition. To demonstrate the impact of negotiation on collaborative activities. To practice intragroup planning and problem-solving processes	Two and one-half to three hours	'79-60

Competition and Collaboration (Win-Lose/Win-Win) (Continued)

Number	Title [Author]	Goals	Time Required	Volume & Page No.
263	**Trading Cards:** A Power Simulation [J. Proescher]	To experience the consequences of conflict between group goals and goals of individual members. To experience intergroup and intragroup competition. To identify patterns of competition and cooperation among group members in a stressful situation. To identify how group and individual strategies affect the group's attainment of a goal	One and one-half to two hours	VII-112
264	**War Gaming:** An Intergroup Competition [A.J. Schuh]	To study group decision making and interaction under stress. To examine the importance of cooperation in small-group work. To demonstrate the effects of win-win and win-lose approaches to intergroup conflict	Two to four hours	VII-117
265	**Monetary Investment:** Negotiation [T. Armor]	To provide insight into the dynamics of negotiation processes: strategy, constituent pressure, consensus, and mediation. To simulate a collective bargaining experience. To explore the behavior of participants in a bargaining situation	One and one-half to two hours	VII-124
278	**Move to Newtown:** A Collaboration Activity [R. Parker & A.H. Hartenstein]	To increase awareness of the dynamics of competition and collaboration. To experience the effects of the use of role power in negotiation situations. To explore the effects of role expectations on behavior and reactions. To practice renegotiation of role responsibilities and expectations within a work unit	A minimum of three hours	'80-60

Competition and Collaboration (Win-Lose/Win-Win) (Continued)

Number	Title [Author]	Goals	Time Required	Volume & Page No.
279	**Creative Products:** Intergroup Conflict Resolution [W.J. Heisler & R.W. Shively]	To examine the effects of collaboration and competition in intergroup relationships. To demonstrate the effects of win-win and win-lose approaches to intergroup conflict. To practice intragroup planning and problem solving	Two and one-half to three hours	'80-69
280	**High Iron:** Collaboration and Competition [D.T. Simpson]	To examine the elements of negotiation and collaboration in achieving goals. To experience the effects of collaboration and/or competition in problem solving	Approximately two hours	'80-78
314	**Territory:** Intergroup Negotiation [P. Cooke & A.J. Reilly]	To experience the effects of a negotiation activity. To increase awareness of various negotiation strategies. To practice collaboration strategies in intergroup problem solving	Approximately two and one-half hours	VIII-120

Collaboration (Win-Win)

Number	Title [Author]	Goals	Time Required	Volume & Page No.
31	**Lutts and Mipps:** Group Problem-Solving [*based on Rimoldi*]	To study the sharing of information in a task-oriented group. To focus on cooperation in group problem solving. To observe the emergence of leadership behavior in group problem solving	Approximately forty-five minutes	II-24

Collaboration (Win-Win) (Continued)

Number	Title [Author]	Goals	Time Required	Volume & Page No.
80	**Energy International:** A Problem-Solving Multiple Role-Play	To study how task-relevant information is shared within a work group. To observe problem-solving strategies within a group. To explore the effects of collaboration and competition in group problem solving	Approximately two hours	'72-25
117	**Pine County:** Information-Sharing [L. Dunn]	To explore the effects of collaboration and competition in group problem solving. To study how task-relevant information is shared within a work group. To observe problem-solving strategies within a group. To demonstrate the impact of various leadership styles on task accomplishment	Approximately one hour	IV-75
133	**Farm E-Z:** A Multiple-Role-Play, Problem-Solving Experience [J.L. Joyce]	To study the sharing of information in task-oriented groups. To learn to distinguish a true problem from those which are only symptomatic. To observe problem-solving strategies within a group	Approximately two hours	'74-44
155	**Sales Puzzle:** Information Sharing [*adapted from A.A. Zoll III*]	To explore the effects of collaboration and competition in group problem solving. To study how information is shared by members of a work group. To observe problem-solving strategies within a group	Approximately one hour	V-34

Collaboration (Win-Win) (Continued)

Number	Title [Author]	Goals	Time Required	Volume & Page No.
156	**Room 703:** Information Sharing [J.R. Joachim]	To explore the effects of collaboration and competition in group problem solving. To study how task-relevant information is shared wihin a work group. To observe group strategies for problem solving	Thirty to forty-five minutes	V-39
284	**Farmers:** Information Sharing [A. Kuperman]	To demonstrate the effects of collaboration and information sharing in problem solving. To explore aspects of collaboration such as verbal communication and division of labor	Approximately two hours	'81-16
302	**Cross-Group Negotiation and Cooperation:** Studying Group Dynamics [B.L. Fisher & R.G. Sachs]	To provide an opportunity to experience the effects of cooperation in task-group functioning. To explore the effects of conflicting objectives on the behavior of members of a task group. To increase awareness of the positive effects of planning, negotiation, and sharing of resources among work-group members	Approximately one and one-half hours	VIII-41

Conflict Resolution/Values Polarization

Number	Title [Author]	Goals	Time Required	Volume & Page No.
14	**Conflict Resolution:** A Collection of Tasks	To generate data about how groups resolve conflict	Varies with each activity	I-70
158	**Absentee:** A Management Role Play [R.J. Carpenter, Jr.]	To explore the dynamics of decision making. To study the resolution and management of conflict. To reveal loyalty patterns among peers and superiors	Approximately one and one-half hours	V-49

Conflict Resolution/Values Polarization (Continued)

Number	Title [Author]	Goals	Time Required	Volume & Page No.
217	**Negotiating Differences:** Avoiding Polarization [D.X. Swenson]	To identify the dimensions along which people may differ. To explore the potential for persons to complement as well as conflict with each other, as a result of such differences. To negotiate a contract for coordinating different personal styles or opinions	Approximately one hour	VI-114
224	**Controversial Issues:** Case Studies in Conflict [J.T. Wood]	To examine the effects of conflict on members of problem-solving groups. To acquaint members with alternative methods of coping with conflict in groups. To examine individual styles of handling conflicts and their effects among members of problem-solving groups	Approximately one and one-half to two hours	'78-28
267	**Whom To Choose:** Values and Group Decision Making [C.L. Eveland & D.M. Hai]	To examine and make choices concerning one's own values. To assess the degree to which members of a group have common values and the impact of this on group decision making. To observe problem-solving strategies in groups	Forty-five minutes to one hour	VII-141

Consensus/Synergy

Number	Title [Author]	Goals	Time Required	Volume & Page No.
11	**Top Problems:** A Consensus-Seeking Task [J.J. Sherwood]	To compare the results of individual decision making with the results of group decision making. To teach effective consensus-seeking behaviors in task groups	Approximately one and one-half hours	I-49

Consensus/Synergy (Continued)

Number	Title [Author]	Goals	Time Required	Volume & Page No.
12	**Choosing a Color:** A Multiple-Role-Play [J.W. Pfeiffer]	To explore behavioral responses to an ambiguous task. To demonstrate the effects of shared leadership	Approximately forty-five minutes	I-56
15	**Residence Halls:** A Consensus-Seeking Task	To study the degree to which members of a group agree on certain values. To assess the decision-making norms of the group. To identify the "natural leadership" functioning in the group	Approximately one hour	I-72
30	**NORC:** A Consensus-Seeking Task [J.E. Jones]	To compare results of individual decision making and of group decision making. To generate data to discuss decision-making patterns in task groups	Approximately one hour	II-18
64	**Kerner Report:** A Consensus-Seeking Task	To compare the results of individual decision making with the results of group decision making. To generate data to discuss decision-making patterns in task groups. To diagnose the level of development in a task group	Approximately one hour	III-64
69	**Supervisory Behavior/ Aims of Education:** Consensus-Seeking Tasks [*worksheets adapted from D. Nylen, J.R. Mitchell, & A. Stout*]	To explore the relationships between subjective involvement with issues and problem solving. To teach effective consensus-seeking behaviors in task groups	Approximately one and one-half hours	III-84
77	**Team Identity** [J.E. Jones]	To develop cohesion within work groups established as part of a larger training group. To explore the dynamics of group task accomplishment	Approximately one and one-half hours	'72-13

Consensus/Synergy (Continued)

Number	Title [Author]	Goals	Time Required	Volume & Page No.
115	**Consensus-Seeking:** A Collection of Tasks [worksheets by D. Keyworth, J.J. Sherwood, J.E. Jones, T. White, M. Carson, B. Rainbow, A. Dew, S. Pavletich, R.D. Jorgenson, & B. Holmberg]	To teach effective consensus-seeking behaviors in task groups. To explore the concept of synergy in reference to outcomes of group decision making	Approximately one hour	IV-51
140	**Lost at Sea:** A Consensus-Seeking Task [P.M. Nemiroff & W.A. Pasmore]	To teach the effectiveness of consensus-seeking behavior in task groups through comparative experiences with both individual decision making and group decision making. To explore the concept of synergy in reference to the outcomes of group decision making	Approximately one hour	'75-28
151	**Cash Register:** Group Decision Making [*based on W.V. Haney*]	To demonstrate how decision making is improved by consensus-seeking. To explore the impact that assumptions have on decision making	Approximately thirty minutes	V-10
157	**Letter Occurrence/ Health Professions Prestige:** Consensus-Seeking Tasks [K.D. Scott & J.W. Pfeiffer]	To compare decisions made by individuals with those made by groups. To teach effective consensus seeking techniques. To demonstrate the phenomenon of synergy	Approximately one hour per task	V-44
177	**Wilderness Survival:** A Consensus-Seeking Task [D.T. Simpson]	To teach effective consensus-seeking behaviors in task groups. To explore the concept of synergy as it relates to outcomes of group decision making	Approximately one and one-half hours	'76-19

Consensus/Synergy (Continued)

Number	Title [Author]	Goals	Time Required	Volume & Page No.
187	**Pyramids:** A Consensus Experience [R.J. Carpenter, Jr.]	To study the consensus process within an organizational hierarchy. To allow participants to define organizational concepts individually and through an organizational process of small-group pyramiding. To explore the dynamics of influence and power within groups and organizations	Approximately two hours	'77-20
223	**Admissions Committee:** A Consensus-Seeking Activity [W.J. Heisler]	To compare decisions made by individuals with those made by groups. To teach effective consensus-seeking techniques. To teach the concept of synergy	Approximately one and one-half to two hours	'78-15
236	**Alphabet Names:** Achieving Synergy in Task Groups [R.P. Greco]	To allow participants to experience the effects of synergy on group tasks. To explore the relationship between group commitment to a task and synergy	Forty-five minutes to one hour	'79-19
255	**Lists:** A Collection of Consensus Activities [B.D. Leskin]	To allow participants to practice giving and receiving feedback. To practice effective consensus-seeking behavior in groups. To demonstrate that relevant performance data from interdependent tasks is widely rather than narrowly shared by group members	Two and one-half to three hours	VII-57
271	**Values for the 1980s:** Consensus Seeking [L.D. Goodstein, W.W. Burke, & P. Cooke]	To provide an opportunity to explore differences between individual and group decision-making processes. To practice consensus-seeking behavior in groups. To explore group members' social values	Approximately three hours	'80-20

ORGANIZATIONS
Awareness/Diagnosis

Number	Title [Author]	Goals	Time Required	Volume & Page No.
40	**Force-Field Analysis:** Individual Problem-Solving [*based on* W.G. Bennis & S. Eisen]	To study dimensions of problems and to devise strategies for solving them through diagram and analysis. To experience the consultative role	Approximately two and one-half hours	II-79
67	**Organizational Mirror:** A Feedback Experience	To generate data that can permit an organization to diagnose its functioning. To establish avenues of feedback between an organization and other groups with which it is linked	Approximately two hours	III-78
73	**Wahoo City:** A Role Alternation [P. Lawson]	To experience the dynamics of an alternate, unaccustomed role in a situation of community (or organization) conflict. To develop skills in conflict resolution, negotiation, and problem solving. To introduce process analysis and feedback as necessary community (or organization) development techniques	A minimum of two hours	III-100
82	**Greeting Cards:** An Organization Simulation	To observe a group's organizational style and functioning. To gather data on individuals' responses to creating and operating a production-centered organization. To give group members feedback on their organizational behavior	Three to six hours	'72-44
98	**Strategies of Changing:** A Multiple-Role-Play [D.J. Marion & A. Edelman; *based on* R. Chin & K.D. Benne]	To acquaint people with three different interpersonal strategies for trying to effect change in human systems	Approximately one hour	'73-32

Awareness/Diagnosis (Continued)

Number	Title [Author]	Goals	Time Required	Volume & Page No.
131	**Roxboro Electric Company:** An OD Role-Play [H. Thomson, with B. Bell, M. Brosseau, P. Fleck, & E. Kahn]	To provide an experience in sensing organizational problems. To provide feedback on interviewing effectiveness. To explore organizational diagnosis and action planning	Approximately two and one-half hours	'74-24
163	**Coloring Book:** An Organization Experiment [*based on M.J. Miller*]	To explore relationships between organizational design and task complexity	Approximately one and one-half hours	V-85
188	**Tug O'War:** A Force-Field Psychodrama [G. Friedrich]	To demonstrate the dynamics in a force-field analysis of a change situation. To involve participants in a problem-solving process	Approximately one hour; one-half hour minimum; repetition with additional problems could take two hours	'77-22
193	**Tri-State:** A Multiple Role Play [H. Karp]	To build skills in diagnosing organizational and group problems. To focus attention on the interrelation between content and process issues	Approximately two and one-half hours	'77-39
194	**Top Secret Contract:** Intergroup Model Building [R.W. Landies & T. Isgar]	To provide a developing or an intact team an experience in the use of newly acquired skills in leadership style, problem solving, decision making, and communication processes. To study group dynamics in a task situation: competition/collaboration, negotiation, confrontation/avoidance, etc. To point out the effect that external influences (outside agents, competition built into the system, production requirements, time and other constraints, etc.) have on team task accomplishment and on individual team members	Approximately two and one-half hours	'77-47

Awareness/Diagnosis (Continued)

Number	Title [Author]	Goals	Time Required	Volume & Page No.
228	**Homesell:** Intergroup Competition [J. Zimmerman]	To explore the ways in which members interact in a work group. To demonstrate different methods of group problem solving. To relate members' group behavior to back-home situations	Approximately three hours. (May be conducted in two sessions of one and one-half hours each)	'78-46

Team Building

Number	Title [Author]	Goals	Time Required	Volume & Page No.
33	**Hollow Square:** A Communications Experiment [W.H. Schmidt & A. Shedlin]	To study dynamics involved in planning a task to be carried out by others. To study dynamics involved in accomplishing a task planned by others. To explore both helpful and hindering communication behaviors in assigning and carrying out a task	Approximately one hour	II-32
68	**Intergroup Meeting:** An Image Exchange	To improve the relationship between two groups, such as levels of management, majority-minority groups, males and females. To explore how groups interact with each other	Three hours	III-81
160	**Tinkertoy Bridge:** Intergroup Competition [G. Bellman]	To analyze individual and team actions in relation to on-the-job experiences. To build awareness of the need for teamwork in completing a task. To demonstrate the effects of competition on team efforts	Approximately one and one-half hours	V-60

Team Building (Continued)

Number	Title [Author]	Goals	Time Required	Volume & Page No.
166	**Agenda Setting:** A Team-Building Starter [J.E. Jones]	To create and rank-order an agenda for a team-building session. To generate ownership of and commitment to commonly perceived problems facing a work group. To develop effective listening skills	Approximately one hour	V-108
171	**Role Clarification:** A Team-Building Activity [J.E. Jones]	To clarify both expectations that team members have of others' roles and conceptions that team members have of their own roles. To promote renegotiation of role responsibilities within a work unit. To teach a process of role adjustment that can become a work-group norm	A minimum of three hours	V-136
232	**MANDOERS:** Organizational Clarification [T.H. Patten, Jr.]	To enable groups undergoing team-building efforts within the same organization to examine management and employee development, organizational effectiveness, and reward systems in the work organization. To explore the diversity of views among participants regarding complex social and behavioral phenomena. To examine feelings resulting from organizational problems and to identify corrective actions that can be taken to deal with them	Two to two and one-half hours	'78-71

Team Building (Continued)

Number	Title [Author]	Goals	Time Required	Volume & Page No.
289	**Intergroup Clearing:** A Relationship-Building Intervention [L.C. Porter]	To "clear the air" between two work groups (departments, divisions, units, teams). To develop intergroup understanding and acceptance. To create the basis for an improved relationship between groups	Approximately three hours	'81-48
297	**Group Effectiveness:** A Team-Building Activity [J.E. Jones & A.J. Reilly]	To increase team members' understanding of the concept of group effectiveness. To generate commitment within an intact group to identify its interaction dynamics	Approximately two hours	VIII-18

Decision Making/Action Planning

Number	Title [Author]	Goals	Time Required	Volume & Page No.
132	**Planning Recommendations or Action:** A Team-Development Guidebook [R.P. Crosby]	To study the process of group decision making. To explore action planning	Approximately three hours	'74-32
244	**What's Important on My Job?:** An Organization Development Activity [D.T. Simpson]	To examine perceptions about sources of motivation in work situations. To experience decision making by group consensus	One and one-half hours. Additional facilitator time is required to conduct a pre-experience survey and tabulate the results	'79-71

Decision Making/Action Planning (Continued)

Number	Volume & Title [Author]	Goals	Time Required	Page No.
259	**Dhabi Fehru:** An MBO Activity [D. Bechtel]	To examine the process of developing task goals for individuals who are working together on a team project. To provide participants an opportunity to practice writing objectives as part of a Management by Objectives training session. To experience the difference between preparing goals for oneself and for others	Three hours	VII-91
275	**Missiles:** Sources of Stress [K.A. Seger]	To identify sources of psychological stress. To demonstrate the effect that individual perceptions of situations have on behavior and decision making under stress. To experience the effects of various types of role power on persons in a decision-making situation	Approximately two hours	'80-43
304	**When to Delegate:** A Manager's Dilemma [T.F. Carney]	To provide an opportunity to exchange views on the topic of delegation. To increase awareness of attitudes about task delegation	Two and one-half to three hours	VIII-52

Conflict Resolution/Values

Number	Title [Author]	Goals	Time Required	Volume & Page No.
144	**Lindell-Billings Corporation:** A Confrontation Role-Play [T.H. Patten, Jr.]	To provide an opportunity to practice confrontation. To explore design considerations in using confrontation inside an organization. To examine and develop skills in intergroup conflict, negotiation, and problem solving	Approximately three hours	'75-46

Conflict Resolution/Values (Continued)

Number	Title [Author]	Goals	Time Required	Volume & Page No.
186	**Conflict Styles:** Organizational Decision Making [D.T. Simpson *based on format by A. Zoll*]	To identify ways of dealing with organizational or group conflict. To discuss when and why different methods of resolving conflict are appropriate to different situations. To provide an experience in group decision making	Approximately one and one-half hours	'77-15
268	**Sexual Values in Organizations:** An OD Role Play [P. Morrison]	To identify a range of personal, ethical, professional, and organizational considerations related to sexual relationships that occur between members of an organization. To determine the effect of such relationships on individual as well as organizational effectiveness	Three hours	VII-146

Consultation Skills

Number	Title [Author]	Goals	Time Required	Volume & Page No.
34	**Hampshire In-Basket:** A Management Activity [J.W. Pfeiffer]	To discover general management principles through personal involvement with problem solving. To examine one's management style. To plan applications of management principles	Approximately three hours	II-41
183	**Consulting Triads:** Self-Assessment [A.G. Banet, Jr.]	To assess consultation skills. To provide practice in one-to-one consultation	Approximately two hours	'76-53
211	**HELPCO:** An OD Role Play [N.E. Rand]	To study the processes of organization development (OD) consultation. To develop OD diagnosis, consultation, and observation skills	Approximately three hours	VI-66

Consultation Skills (Continued)

Number	Title [Author]	Goals	Time Required	Volume & Page No.
230	**Willington:** An Intervention-Skills Role Play [W.A. Randolph, J.C. Ferrie, & D.D Palmer]	To determine the appropriate intervention strategy for a simulated organization. To implement a strategy for entering, initially diagnosing, and contracting with the simulated organization. To provide feedback on the consulting team members' intervention skills and strategy. To explore theory, skills, values, and strategies of organization development (OD)	Two and one-half to three hours	'78-55

FACILITATING LEARNING
Getting Acquainted

Number	Title [Author]	Goals	Time Required	Volume & Page No.
1	**Listening and Inferring:** A Getting-Acquainted Activity	To facilitate the involvement of individuals in a newly formed group	Fifteen minutes	I-3
5	**Who Am I?:** A Getting-Acquainted Activity	To allow participants to become acquainted quickly in a relatively non-threatening way	Approximately forty-five minutes	I-19
49	**"Who Am I?" Variations:** A Getting-Acquainted Activity	To allow participants to become acquainted quickly in a non-threatening way	Approximately forty-five minutes	III-3
101	**Getting Acquainted:** A Potpourri	To be used as ice breakers in human relations training events	Varies with each listed experience	IV-3
245	**Tea Party:** An Ice Breaker [D. Keyworth]	To allow participants to share experiences and perceptions in a non-threatening manner. To promote acquaintance and a feeling of interaction in a new group	Fifteen minutes to one hour	VII-5

Getting Acquainted (Continued)

Number	Volume & Title [Author]	Goals	Time Required	Page No.
269	**Autographs:** An Ice Breaker [J.E. Jones]	To facilitate the getting-acquainted process in a large group. To alleviate anxiety experienced during the beginning of a training session	Approximately one-half hour	'80-11
281	**Alliterative Names:** A Getting-Acquainted Activity	To facilitate the getting-acquainted process in a small group. To promote self-disclosure in a new group	Approximately one-half hour	'81-9
282	**Birth Signs:** An Ice Breaker [J.E. Jones]	To facilitate the getting-acquainted process in a large group. To alleviate participants' anxiety at the beginning of a training session	Approximately one-half hour	'81-11
293	**Name Tags:** An Ice Breaker [D. Martin & C. Cherrey]	To provide participants with an opportunity to introduce themselves in a nonthreatening and enjoyable manner. To develop an atmosphere conducive to group interaction	Fifteen minutes	VIII-5
294	**Learning Exchange:** A Getting-Acquainted Activity [A.F. Farquharson]	To provide an opportunity for participants to get to know each other. To demonstrate the knowledge and skills that the participants have brought to the group. To raise awareness of factors that enhance the teaching-learning process	Approximately one hour	VIII-7
295	**People on the Job:** Expressing Opinions [M.B. Ross]	To afford participants the opportunity to share their views in a structured environment. To provide a sense of the variety of opinions and attitudes that exist about a particular subject. To develop a climate for future group interaction	One and one-half to two hours	VIII-10

Forming Subgroups

Number	Title [Author]	Goals	Time Required	Volume & Page No.
2	Two-Four-Eight: Building Teams	To divide a large group into workable subgroups in such a way as to increase group cohesiveness and identity	Approximately thirty minutes	I-5
27	Jigsaw: Forming Groups	To establish group cohesion by forming a large number of participants into groups with pre-determined compositions	Approximately thirty minutes	II-10
51	Empty Chair: An Extended Group Design	To allow all participants to become involved voluntarily in a group-on-group experience when the size of the total group makes discussion impractical	Open	III-8
125	Hum-Dinger: A Getting-Acquainted Activity [A.D. Duncan]	To break a large group into smaller groups in a nonthreatening manner. To facilitate contact between all members of a large group in a related climate of fun and humor	Approximately thirty minutes	'74-7
173	Limericks: Getting Acquainted [E. Racicot]	To acquaint and involve participants with one another through non-threatening physical activity. To divide a large group into subgroups in a climate of humor and cohesiveness	Approximately thirty minutes	'76-7

Expectations of Learners/Facilitators

Number	Title [Author]	Goals	Time Required	Volume & Page No.
91	Perception of Task: A Teaching-Learning Exercise [R.T. Williams]	To examine how perceptions of a learning task by teacher and learner influence teaching styles and learning styles	One hour	'73-15

Expectations of Learners/Facilitators (Continued)

Number	Title [Author]	Goals	Time Required	Volume & Page No.
96	Participant-Staff Expectations [A.H. Munoz]	To provide participants and facilitators the opportunity to examine and discuss mutual expectations and perceptions regarding the training program. To reduce the "expectation gap" between participants and facilitators	Approximately one hour	'73-29

Dealing with Blocks to Learning

Number	Title [Author]	Goals	Time Required	Volume & Page No.
42	First Names, First Impressions: A Feedback Experience [J.E. Jones]	To get acquainted with other members of a small group. To discover one's initial impact on others. To study phenomena related to first impressions—their accuracy and effects	Approximately one hour	II-88
43	Verbal Activities Within Groups: A Potpourri	To be used as openers when meetings of the groups are infrequent, or may be used as interventions within meetings	Varies with each activity	II-91
87	Peter-Paul: Getting Acquainted [E.L. Solley]	To help group members get acquainted quickly in a relatively nonthreatening manner. To explore feelings generated by "becoming another person." To explore the dimensions of a brief encounter. To emphasize the need for careful, active listening during conversation	Minimum of ten minutes plus two minutes per group member	'73-7

Dealing with Blocks to Learning (Continued)

Number	Title [Author]	Goals	Time Required	Volume & Page No.
89	**Gunnysack:** An Introduction to Here-and-Now [J.E. Jones]	To establish the norm of attending to here-and-now data and "gunnysacking" then-and-there data. To help participants to become aware of their own here-and-now reactions	Approximately thirty minutes	'73-11
106	**Sculpturing:** An Expression of Feelings [L.A. McKeown, B. Kaye, R. McLean, & J. Linhardt]	To provide a nonverbal medium for the expression of feelings toward another person. To promote feedback on individual behavior	Approximately forty-five minutes	IV-21
112	**The "T" Test:** An Experiential Lecture on Traits [A.J. Reilly]	To introduce the concept of personality traits. To illustrate the process of inferring characteristics from behavior. To help diminish some of the unproductive anxiety which is often associated with filling out psychological instruments or inventories	Approximately thirty minutes	IV-41
145	**Win What, Lose What?:** An Intergroup Conflict Intervention [K. Finn]	To examine the elements of intergroup conflict. To illustrate a process of conflict resolution	Approximately three hours	'75-51
191	**Communication Analysis:** A Getting-Acquainted Activity [R.D. Jorgenson]	To establish a laboratory-learning climate in the initial stages of a group composed of hostile or reluctant participants. To experience openness in exploring positive and negative feelings in a non-threatening atmosphere. To examine how affective elements (especially negative feelings) influence the result of communication	Approximately one hour	'77-32

Dealing with Blocks to Learning (Continued)

Number	Title [Author]	Goals	Time Required	Volume & Page No.
301	Resistance to Learning: Developing New Skills [H. Bracey & R. Trueblood]	To provide a model for understanding the phenomenon of behavioral resistance in learning situations. To demonstrate various behavioral mainfestations of resistance. To increase awareness of techniques that can be used to overcome resistance in learning situations	Two hours	VIII-37

Building Trust

Number	Title [Author]	Goals	Time Required	Volume & Page No.
45	Helping Pairs: A Collection	To build helping relationships ancillary to small-group experiences. To give participants an opportunity to try out new behavior within a dyadic relationship. To provide group members with ways of checking out their perceptions of and reactions to laboratory experiences	Varies with each activity	II-97
90	Make Your Own Bag: Symbolic Self-Disclosure [C. Lawson]	To raise levels of trust and openness in a group. To make group members aware of themselves and others as persons	Approximately one hour and forty-five minutes	'73-13
120	Dimensions of Trust: A Symbolic Expression [J. Costigan]	To explore the various dimensions and meanings of trust. To promote the creative expression of trust	Approximately one hour	IV-96

Building Trust (Continued)

Number	Title [Author]	Goals	Time Required	Volume & Page No.
196	Current Status: A Feedback Activity on Trust [R.N. Glenn]	To examine unexpressed feelings of trust or distrust within an ongoing group and to clarify the reasons for these feelings. To increase feelings of trust within the group. To promote self-disclosure and risk taking. To provide a basis for subsequent assessment of group trust	Approximately one and one-half hours	'77-57

Building Norms of Openness

Number	Title [Author]	Goals	Time Required	Volume & Page No.
25	Group Conversation: Discussion-Starters [D. Castle]	To develop a compatible climate and readiness for interaction in a group through sharing personal experience	Can be a fifteen-minute preface to other group activities or planned for an entire meeting	II-3
88	"Cold" Introductions: Getting Acquainted [J.E. Jones]	To help participants to get to know each other while building expectations of risk taking and receptivity to feedback. To build norms of openness, experimentation, and attention to process	Approximately three minutes per participant	'73-9
93	Building Open and Closed Relationships [adapted from W. Barber]	To enable group members to focus on the elements of relationships which characterize them as open or closed. To facilitate the cohesiveness of personal growth or otherwise-designated groups who will be working together	One and one-half to two hours	'73-20

Building Norms of Openness (Continued)

Number	Title [Author]	Goals	Time Required	Volume & Page No.
109	**Growth Cards:** Experimenting with New Behavior [M. Cahn]	To develop an accepting atmosphere for risk taking and self-disclosure. To give those within a larger laboratory community a legitimate entry point for the provision of individual feedback to participants in other groups. To supply participants with specific, individual feedback to aid them in making decisions concerning an agenda for modifying their own behavior. To increase understanding and acceptance of personality components which decrease interpersonal effectiveness. To strengthen individual commitment to behavioral change through open verbalization and the development of a method or prescription for modification. To reinforce group skills of decision making and task performance	Approximately two hours	IV-30
129	**Forced-Choice Identity:** A Self-Disclosure Activity [J.J. Sherwood]	To gain insight about oneself. To facilitate self-disclosure and feedback. To encourage community-building. To enhance enjoyment of the group experience through a change-of-pace activity	Approximately two hours	'74-20
174	**Labeling:** A Getting-Acquainted Activity [C.L. Kormanski]	To provide opportunities to become acquainted with other members of the group. To promote feedback and self-disclosure among participants regarding initial perceptions	Approximately one hour	'76-10

Building Norms of Openness (Continued)

Number	Title [Author]	Goals	Time Required	Volume & Page No.
197	**Best Friend:** A Getting-Acquainted Activity [D.L. Garris]	To afford participants the opportunity to introduce themselves in a non-threatening manner. To develop a climate for group interaction by sharing personal information	Approximately forty-five minutes	VI-3
246	**Personal Identity:** An Ice Breaker [D.E. Whiteside]	To enable participants to "try on" new identities. To explore the influence of a different identity on the behavior of others. To explore the relationship between honesty and trust	Approximately one hour	VII-11

Energizers

Number	Title [Author]	Goals	Time Required	Volume & Page No.
149	**Energizers:** Group Starters	To prepare participants for meetings	Varies with each activity	V-3

Evaluating Learning-Group Process

Number	Title [Author]	Goals	Time Required	Volume & Page No.
24	**Assumptions About Human Relations Training:** An Opinnionaire [J.E. Jones; worksheets by J. Dickinson, C. Dee, J.E. Jones, & B.H. Arbes]	To allow the group to assess the degree to which it has consensus on a number of assumptions that underlie laboratory learning. To assist co-facilitators in identifying each other's biases about training. To discover some possible "blind spots" that the training staff may have about training	Minimum of one hour	I-107

Evaluating Learning-Group Process (Continued)

Number	Title [Author]	Goals	Time Required	Volume & Page No.
55	**Group Self-Evaluations:** A Collection of Instruments	To help a group evaluate its own functioning. To provide a way to examine objectively the participation of group members. To explore the norms that have developed in a group which has been meeting for some time	Varies according to the evaluative procedures used	III-22
74	**Personal Journal:** A Self-Evaluation	To heighten participants' awareness of the sequence of events and the corresponding emotional development which takes place in a laboratory or a workshop. To aid in self-disclosure	Any number of periods of ten to fifteen minutes each, depending on the design of the laboratory or workshop	III-109
85	**Growth and Name Fantasy** [A.G. Banet, Jr.]	To provide group participants with an opportunity to review, in fantasy, the phases of growth and development they have accomplished. To review their sense of individual identity	Approximately forty-five minutes	'72-59
92	**Medial Feedback:** A "Mid-Course Correction" Exercise	To generate evaluative data about the effects of a laboratory education design while there is still time to modify it. To study group process phenomena both as a participant and as an observer	Approximately one and one-half hours	'73-17
182	**The Other You:** Awareness Expansion [A.J. Reilly]	To increase personal self-awareness. To provide participants an opportunity to experiment with new behavior. To help participants integrate new data into their self-concepts	Approximately two and one-half hours	'76-51

Evaluating Learning-Group Process (Continued)

Number	Title [Author]	Goals	Time Required	Volume & Page No.
214	**Roles Impact Feelings:** A Role Play [M. Smith]	To enable participants to become aware of some of the roles they play. To discover how roles produce feelings	Approximately two and one-half hours	VI-102
234	**Buttermilk:** Awareness Expansion [T.R. Harvey]	To demonstrate the processes of interpersonal influence and personal change. To "warm up" groups that are interested in exploring the dynamics of change	One-half hour	'79-13

Developing Group Facilitator Skills

Number	Title [Author]	Goals	Time Required	Volume & Page No.
26	**Miniversity: Sharing Participants' Ideas**	To provide for dissemination of information, using participants as resources, during a conference, workshop, or institute	Time is dependent on the size of the group, the facilities available, and the number of "courses" offered	II-7
47	**Microlab:** A Training Demonstration	To demonstrate human relations training methods. To accelerate the development of growth-producing norms, such as openness and attention to feelings	Depends on variations employed in the design	II-113
48	**Process Intervention:** A Facilitator Practice Session	To provide practice in intervening in small groups. To generate feedback on intervention styles	At least one hour	II-115

Developing Group Facilitator Skills (Continued)

Number	Title [Author]	Goals	Time Required	Volume & Page No.
148	**Group Leadership Functions:** A Facilitator-Style Activity [R.K. Conyne]	To explore four basic leadership functions of group facilitators. To study the relationship between leadership functions and general interpersonal style	Approximately two hours	'75-63
172	**Group Composition:** A Selection Activity [G.M. Phillips & A.G. Banet, Jr.]	To explore the process of selection of group members. To assist facilitators in identifying their biases about group composition. To study similarities and differences between personal growth and psychotherapy groups	Approximately one and one-half hours	V-139

Closure

Number	Title [Author]	Goals	Time Required	Volume & Page No.
86	**Symbolic Closing Exercise** [M. Smith]	To finish a workshop or laboratory with a sense of closure. To re-enact the group process in symbolic nonverbal action	Approximately ten minutes	'72-61
114	**Closure:** Variations on a Theme	To be useful in closing human relations training events. Can also be employed to foster self-disclosure in personal growth groups	Varies with each idea	IV-49
176	**Symbolic Toast:** A Closure Experience [A.D. Duncan & J.F. Dorris]	To provide closure at the end of a training experience. To provide an opportunity for participants to give and receive feedback. To allow each person to receive some personal validation from each member of the group. To affirm the personal strengths of the participants	Approximately forty minutes	'76-17

Closure (Continued)

Number	Title [Author]	Goals	Time Required	Volume & Page No.
201	**Bread Making:** An Integrating Experience [A.G. Banet, Jr.]	To experience collaborating on an unusual group task. To focus on the sensory, fantasy, and creative aspects of food preparation. To provide a sensory, nonverbal background for integrating learning in the final stages of a workshop	Approximately one hour and twenty minutes (One sixty-minute period followed by one twenty-minute period later on)	VI-19
222	**Golden Awards:** A Closure Activity [J. Elliott-Kemp & G. Williams]	To provide an opportunity for group and self-appraisal. To allow members a chance to see how others perceive them. To practice giving feedback to others in a constructive and helpful manner	Approximately two hours	'78-12

INTRODUCTION TO INSTRUMENTS

Instruments can be used in a number of ways by group facilitators. Data from inventories can be interpreted normatively or intrapersonally, but it is important that they be coordinated carefully with the goals of the training design. Some uses of instrumentation include the following:

Providing instrumented feedback to group members. Participants complete, score, and interpret their own scales. They can be asked to predict each other's scores. They can fill out scales for each other as feedback.

Manipulating group composition. For brief, experimental demonstrations of the effects of group composition, various mixes of group members can be established. Long-term groups can be built that offer the promise of beneficial outcomes. Extremes of both homogeneity and heterogeneity can be avoided.

Teaching theory of interpersonal functioning. Some brief instruments are intended primarily to introduce concepts. Participants are involved with theory by investing in an activity such as completing an inventory related to the model being explored.

Researching outcomes of training interventions. Even scales with relatively low reliability can be effective in the study of group phenomena when used with pretest or follow-up procedures.

Studying here-and-now process in groups. It is sometimes helpful to use an instrument to assist the group in diagnosing its own internal functioning. The data can be focused on what is happening and what changes are desirable.

DISADVANTAGES AND ADVANTAGES OF USING INSTRUMENTS[1]

It is important to note both the advantages and the disadvantages of using instruments in human relations training.

Disadvantages

One of the key disadvantages of using instruments is that people often fear that someone has, so to speak, obtained an indelible fingerprinting of them, that they have been exposed, that somebody has read their minds. It is important for facilitators using instruments to reduce this tendency to overstate the accuracy and stability of an instrument.

Another disadvantage is that instruments tend to encourage participants to be dependent on the facilitator, thus locating the leadership (control) of the group with the facilitator rather than allowing it to be shared among the members.

The use of instruments can be a means of dissipating the useful tension of person-to-person encounter, especially in a personal growth workshop. Both the participants

---

[1]The following discussion on the disadvantages and advantages of using instruments is based on J. William Pfeiffer, Richard Heslin, and John E. Jones, *Instrumentation in Human Relations Training* (2nd ed.), San Diego, CA: University Associates, 1976, pp. 11-17.

and the leader may be denied some of the ambiguous but potentially growth-inducing tension produced by face-to-face encounter and reactions to one another.

Instruments often generate a rash of nit-picking responses in which the participants question the items, reliability, validity, or relevance of an instrument. Much valuable time can be used in arguing about the instrument itself. Nit-picking is often a result of the fact that the participant has received information that disburbs him and fears that this profile is irrevocably "him" or that people are going to interpret his data in a negative fashion.

Instruments also have the potential for generating significant hostility from participants who may see them as irrelevant, time consuming, and, in general, diverting attention from the key issues of the workshop. This may be attributable in part to a preconceived notion that "structure" is not an appropriate part of group experience, particularly in a personal growth group.

Finally, instruments can supply a person with more feedback than he is ready to handle; that is, an instrument can overload him with information that he does not have time to assimilate, to work through, to put into perspective.

Avoiding the Disadvantages

A number of the disadvantages mentioned can be avoided by removing the mysticism surrounding instruments. Effort should be made to prevent people from assuming that an instrument is an error-free, God-directed opening of the soul to everyone. Rather, participants should be encouraged to view instrumented experiences like any other choice-making experience in their everyday lives. They have given answers to a lot of situations described in the instrument, added up those answers, and come up with a score. If they have trouble understanding where the score came from, they should be encouraged to go back to each item fed into the score, examine how they responded to each item and how they scored it, and perhaps compare their responses to other people's—item by item, response by response, and situation by situation.

A second way to avoid some of the disadvantages of instruments is to make sure that individuals have sufficient time to process what the instrument has revealed about them. Each participant should be given an opportunity to talk through his scores, to compare his scores in detail with those of others in the group, and to discuss why he sees life from a different perspective than some of the other participants. He may also discuss how his view of his scores reflects his personal orientation and may compare this with some other people's orientations.

Advantages

Instrumented approaches give a recipient early opportunities to understand the theory involved in the dynamics of his own group situation—an understanding that will increase his involvement. By judicious choice of an appropriate instrument during the first group session, the facilitator can quickly offer the participant a theory about personality style, group development, interpersonal relations, or leadership that he can use throughout the rest of the group experience.

Another advantage of using instruments is that they give the participant some constructs and terminology early in the group experience that he can use in looking at his and other people's behavior and in categorizing and describing what goes on between individuals or within an individual. A related advantage is that the person forms a commitment to the information, constructs, and theory that he has been given, because his instrumented feedback describes him in terms of these constructs. One way of tying a person's ego to some useful theory about groups and interpersonal relations is to give the theory personal impact.

Another advantage is that a participant can be given feedback about his personal behavior early in a group experience. It often happens in a workshop that a person does not get feedback about his style or about the way he relates to other participants until the last day, the last meeting, or the last two or three hours of the workshop. It may take that long before the other participants have developed the skills necessary to give effective feedback to someone and before an atmosphere of trust can be developed in the group so that members can feel comfortable in giving that kind of feedback to another member. Regardless of the causes of this situation, the person then has some information about himself with no time to work on new behavior that might modify the aspect of himself that has been described. Instruments administered early in the group experience help to compensate for the lack of feedback from others by giving a person some information about his style, his perceptual framework toward other people, and the way others react to him. Thus, he can generate an agenda of behavior modification for himself on the characteristics uncovered by the instrument while he still has the remainder of the workshop to work on them.

Instruments surface latent issues that should be dealt with in the group setting. This is true whether the issues and problems are within an individual, between individuals, or within an organization. By administering an instrument that uncovers these issues, the facilitator makes these issues public, i.e., outside the individual or the organization. They then become legitimate materials to deal with, to discuss, to try to correct, or to improve.

Instruments give feedback to an individual or an organization in a way that is characterized by relatively low threat. That is, when a person gets information from a questionnaire that he has filled out himself, he is more likely to trust that data than data he receives from another individual about his personal style. At least he does not have the dilemma of trying to sort out whether the information is mostly a function of his behavior, of the perceptual framework of the person who is giving him the feedback, or of some chemistry that exists between the two of them. He can be fairly sure that the instrument holds no personal malevolence toward him; therefore, he can be freer to accept the information, understanding the fact that the information actually came from his own responses to descriptions of situations.

Another advantage is that instruments not only give feedback about the individual, but they also allow him to compare himself with others. We all are aware that we may be more or less dominating than other people, that we may enjoy being with people more or less than others, that we may have a greater or lesser need for people to like us, and so on. However, it is often an eye-opening experience to find out that we are stronger in one or more of our characteristics than ninety-nine percent of the people in a certain norm group. This last piece of information, indicating that a person ranks not only high on a characteristic, but *unusually* high, may cause a person to pause and examine carefully whether this characteristic is becoming dysfunctional for him, e.g., getting in the way of his performance on the job or at home.

An advantage of instruments for the facilitator of small groups is that they allow him to focus the energies and time of the participants on the most appropriate material and also to control, to some extent, the matters that are dealt with in the workshop. In this way he is able to ensure that the issues worked on are crucial, existing ones rather than less important ones that the members may introduce to avoid grappling with the more uncomfortable issues.

A final advantage is that instruments allow longitudinal assessment of change in a group, an organization, or an individual. This assessment can be useful in organization development for demonstrating that the group interventions in which the organization is involved are compatible with the goals the consultant has determined from sensing efforts and/or compatible with the stated goals of the organization. This advantage is valuable in terms of group research and also for personal goal feedback.

SUMMARY

The Use of Instrumentation in Small Groups

Disadvantages	Advantages
Engenders fear of exposure	Enables early, easy theory learning
Fosters dependency on the facilitator	Develops early understanding of constructs and terminology
Relieves potentially growthful tension	Produces personal commitment to information, theory, and constructs
Generates time-consuming nit-picking	Supplies early personal feedback
May be seen as diverting from key issues and may arouse hostility	Surfaces latent issues
Can result in overload of feedback	Fosters open reception of feedback through low threat
	Provides for comparisons of individuals with norm groups
	Allows facilitator to focus and control group appropriately
	Facilitates longitudinal assessment of change

Avoiding the Disadvantages of Instruments

1. The facilitator can make a concerted effort to remove the mysticism surrounding instrumentation:
    a. By discussing the margin of error and other factors that contribute to less-than-absolute results.
    b. By allowing and encouraging participants to explore the instrument thoroughly so that they see how it was designed and how their scores were derived.
    c. By showing participants how instrumentation is related to everyday, choice-making experiences.
2. The facilitator can ensure that sufficient time is made available for processing the data:
    a. By giving participants an opportunity to talk through their scores and to compare their scores with others.
    b. By emphasizing and legitimizing the differing life perspectives and orientations of people.

SEVEN PHASES IN USING AN INSTRUMENT

Using an instrument properly, that is, obtaining the best possible value from it, entails seven different phases: (1) administration; (2) theory input; (3) prediction; (4) scoring; (5) interpretation; (6) posting; and (7) processing.

In the first step, *administration,* a nonthreatening atmosphere should be established and the purposes of the instrument discussed. In larger groups particularly, the administrator may need to tell those individuals who finish first to wait quietly for the others to finish.

Next, the facilitator should take a few minutes to give the participants some *theory input* for the instrument by explaining the rationale behind its use.

Each participant should be asked to make a *prediction* about his score(s) by estimating whether he will score high, medium, or low and by recording his estimate.

Scoring can be done in a number of ways. Some instruments require templates, some are self-scoring, and some require that scores be announced, written on newsprint, or handed out on a mimeographed sheet. The sophistication of the particular group is a gauge of the most appropriate method of scoring. Sometimes it is more efficient for the facilitator or an assistant to do the scoring than to have participants do it. In this way, of course, individuals do not get instant feedback, but often the instrument can be administered before a meal break and the results made available immediately after the break. The essential guideline in scoring is that it should not detract from the data being generated.

The manner in which *interpretation* is handled may vary widely, depending on the group and the style of the facilitator. One suggested way is to use two stages: (1) an interpretation of the administrator's (or another staff member's) scores, and then (2) an interpretation between pairs of participants. Thus, participants can first see how interpretations are made. Also, if staff members are willing to share their scores, participants find it less threatening to share theirs.

The sixth phase is *posting*. Displaying scores on newsprint can dissipate some people's concerns about possible negative values attached to their scores. At the same time, it can generate additional useful data for the group. Posting scores for discussion is particularly effective in subgroups.

The final, and perhaps most crucial, phase of instrumentation is *processing*. Group processing can simultaneously defuse negative affect and promote integration of the data concepts. Six to twelve participants form a group of ideal size for processing.

WHAT TO LOOK FOR IN AN INSTRUMENT

In examining the training applications and use of instruments, we have identified some dimensions that need to be considered in selecting or assessing an instrument. The following chart reflects our judgment of the relative amount of concern each dimension warrants in training, organizational survey, personnel selection, and research applications.

	INSTRUMENTATION APPLICATION			
DIMENSION	**Training**	**Organizational Assessment**	**Personnel Selection**	**Research**
Validity* Are the data useful?	High	High	High	High
Reliability How accurate or stable are the scores?	Medium	Medium	Medium	High
Objectivity Is the scoring dependent on the judgments of the scorer, or is there a standard key?	High	High	High	Medium
Theoretical base Is the instrument based on a viable model?	High	High	Low	High

---

*Validity takes on different meanings in these four contexts. In *training* the validity of the scale is in the user; that is, "Can I use this scale to help participants in training learn more effective behavior?" In *organizational assessment* the overriding consideration is: "Does this instrument tap those process dimensions that are correlated with production?" In *personnel selection* the use of instruments centers around predictive—or discriminative—validity: "Is this instrument significantly related to a meaningful success criterion?" In *research* the major concern is the theoretical constructs being measured: "Does this scale measure the concepts derived from theory sufficiently well to permit meaningful tests of hypotheses derived from the model used?" Validity is always situation-specific; it resides not so much in the instrument as in the particular use of it.

INSTRUMENTATION APPLICATION

DIMENSION	Training	Organizational Assessment	Personnel Selection	Research
Behavioral orientation Are the scores derived from the respondents' descriptions of their behavior?	High	High	Low	Low
Observability Can the scores be related to the observable behavior of respondents?	High	Medium	Low	Low
Language Is the instrument written at an appropriate reading level? Does it use a special vocabulary or jargon?	High	High	High	High
Special training How much professional preparation is required to use the scale?	High	High	High	High
Adaptability Can the items be adapted/amended to fit a particular situation?	Medium	High	Low	Low
Copyright restrictions Can it be photo-reproduced or edited without special permission?	High	Medium	Medium	Medium
Transparency How obvious is the rationale underlying the items?	Low	Low	High	Medium
Fakeability How easy is it for respondents to manipulate their scores?	Low	Medium	High	Medium
Norms Are relevant norms available?	Low	Low	High	Medium
Time required How much time is needed to prepare, administer, score, and interpret the instrument?	High	High	Low	Medium
Expense What is the cost of the materials, scoring, analyses, and background documents? Are these reusable materials?	Medium	High	Medium	Medium

DIMENSION	INSTRUMENTATION APPLICATION			
	Training	Organizational Assessment	Personnel Selection	Research
Accessibility Are the materials readily available?	Medium	Medium	Medium	Medium
Special materials Does the instrument require that any special apparatus be set up in advance?	High	Medium	Medium	Medium
Noxiousness Would the items—or the scale itself—offend intended respondents?	High	High	Medium	High
Scoring complexity Can the instrument be self-scored? Are electronic/clerical options available?	High	Low	Medium	Low
Data reduction How many scores are derived? Can these be summarized for ease in interpretation?	High	High	Medium	Low
Handouts Are easily read interpretive materials available to be distributed to respondents?	Medium	Medium	Low	Low
Familiarity How likely is it that participants will have responded to the scale before?	Low	Low	Medium	High

CLASSIFICATION OF INSTRUMENTS

The sixty-six paper-and-pencil assessment devices that have appeared in the *Handbooks* and the *Annuals* are categorized in the following section, using the following classifications:

> Personal
> Interpersonal
> Management/Leadership Style
> Organizations
> Group Behavior.

PERSONAL

Title	Author(s)	Volume & Page No.
Dependency-Intimacy Rating Form	J.E. Jones	I-84
Life-Planning Program		II-103
Learning-Climate Analysis Form		III-36
Group-Behavior Questionnaire		III-39
Intentions and Choices Inventory		III-40
Polarization: Opinionnaire on Womanhood	J.E. Jones & J.J. Jones	III-61
Sex-Role Stereotyping Rating Scale	M. Carson	'73-28
Johari Window Self-Rating Sheet	P.G. Hanson	'73-41
Motivation Feedback Opinionnaire	D.F. Michalak	'73-44
The Involvement Inventory	R. Heslin & B. Blake	'73-87
Self-Disclosure Questionnaire	S.M. Jourard	'74-103
Risk-Taking Behavior in Groups Questionnaire	R.R. Kurtz	IV-110
Inventory of Self-Actualizing Characteristics (ISAC)	A.G. Banet, Jr.	'76-67
Bem Sex-Role Inventory (BSRI)	S.L. Bem	'77-83
Mach V Attitude Inventory	R. Christie	'78-95
Satisfaction Survey: An Affective Personal Feedback Instrument	A.J. Schuh	'79-85
Personal Style Inventory	R.C. Hogan & D.W. Champagne	'80-89

INTERPERSONAL

Title	Author(s)	Volume & Page No.
Interpersonal Relationship Rating Scale	J.L. Hipple	'72-69
Helping Relationship Inventory	J.E. Jones; *adapted from E.H. Porter*	'73-53
Scale of Feelings and Behavior of Love	C.H. Swensen & F. Gilner	'73-71
Interpersonal Communication Inventory	M.J. Bienvenu, Sr.	'74-97
Scale of Marriage Problems	C.H. Swensen & A. Fiore	'75-71
Inventory of Anger Communication (IAC)	M.J. Bienvenu, Sr.	'76-79
Interpersonal Check List (ICL)	R. LaForge	'77-89
Role Efficacy Scale	U. Pareek	'80-100

MANAGEMENT/LEADERSHIP STYLE

Title	Author(s)	Volume & Page No.
T-P Leadership Questionnaire	*adapted from Sergiovanni, Metzcus, and Burden*	I-10
Supervisory Attitudes: The X-Y Scale	*adapted from R.N. Ford*	'72-65
Intervention Style Survey	B.H. Arbes	'72-75
LEAD (Leadership: Employee-Orientation and Differentiation Questionnaire	R. Doré	'73-95
S-C (Student-Content) Teaching Inventory	M.S. Spier	'74-113
Decision-Style Inventory	R. Roskin	'75-89
Leader Effectiveness and Adaptability Description (LEAD)	P. Hersey & K.H. Blanchard	'76-87
Phases of Integrated Problem Solving (PIPS)	W.C. Morris & M. Sashkin	'78-105
Women as Managers Scale (WAMS)	J.R. Terborg	'79-79
Training Style Inventory (TSI)	R. Brostrom	'79-92
Increasing Employee Self-Control (IESC)	B.H. Harvey	'80-106
When to Delegate Inventory Sheet	T.F. Carney	VIII-55
Patterns of Effective Supervisory Behavior	H.P. Sims, Jr.	'81-95

ORGANIZATIONS

Title	Author(s)	Volume & Page No.
Force-Field Analysis Inventory	*based on W.G. Bennis & S. Eisen*	II-82
Group-Climate Inventory		III-25
Team-Building: Sensing Interview Guide	J.E. Jones	III-76
Problem-Analysis Questionnaire	B. Oshry & R. Harrison	'75-81
Diagnosing Organization Ideology	R. Harrison	'75-101
Organization Behavior Describer Survey (OBDS)	R. Harrison & B. Oshry	'76-101
Organizational Norms Opinionnaire	M. Alexander	'78-81
Critical Consulting Incidents Inventory (CCII)	J.E. Jones & A.G. Banet, Jr.	'78-89
OD Readiness Check List	J.W. Pfeiffer & J.E. Jones	'78-226
Power and OD Intervention Analysis (PODIA)	M. Sashkin & J.E. Jones	'79-99
Sexual Values in Organizations Questionnaire	P. Morrison & R. DeGraw	VII-150
Organizational Diagnosis Questionnaire (ODQ)	R.C. Preziosi	'80-112
People on the Job Work Sheet	M.B. Ross	VIII-13
Organizational-Process Survey	F. Burns & R.L. Gragg	'81-92
Diagnosing Organizational Conflict-Management Climates	B. Crosby & J.J. Scherer	'81-100

GROUP BEHAVIOR

Title	Author(s)	Volume & Page No.
Opinionnaire on Assumptions About Human Relations Training	J.E. Jones, J. Dickinson, & C. Dee	I-110
Group-Growth Evaluation Form		III-26
Feedback Rating Scales		III-28
Postmeeting Reactions Form		III-30
Nonresearch Uses of the Group Leadership Questionnaire (GTQ-C)	D.B. Wile	'72-87
Reactions to Group Situations Test	H.A. Thelen	'74-89
Group Leadership Functions Scale	R.K. Conyne	'75-65
Group Leader Self-Disclosure Scale	R.R. Dies	'77-65

GROUP BEHAVIOR (Continued)

Title	Author(s)	Volume & Page No.
TORI Group Self-Diagnosis Scale	J.R. Gibb	'77-73
The Group Incidents Questionnaire (GIQ): A Measure of Skill in Group Facilitation	J.P. Stokes & R.C. Tait	'81-75
Meeting-Evaluation Scale	F. Burns & R.L. Gragg	'81-89
Work-Group-Effectiveness Inventory	F. Burns & R.L. Gragg	'81-90
Learning-Group Process Scale	F. Burns & R.L. Gragg	'81-94

INTRODUCTION TO LECTURETTES

Learning based on direct experience is not the only kind of learning appropriate to human relations training. Contrary to some criticisms of the field, group facilitators are not exclusively concerned with "gut-involved" experience; "head" learning is also valued.

"Anti-Head" Bias

There is, however, a persistent "anti-head" bias within the field. This anti-theoretical, anti-cognitive, anti-didactic, anti-role bias may cause many participants, as well as facilitators, to discount or undervalue cognitive input in a laboratory experience. Participants often do not want a *lecture;* they would rather talk about their feelings or stress their concerns for practicality. Some facilitators thus may neglect the support that theoretical material can provide. Our bias is clearly for the practical application of theory and research to laboratory training. "Gut" experience and "head" learning can support, alter, validate, extend, and complement each other. Both affective and cognitive data are important in human relations training.

Lecture Method

Although the lecture method can easily be overused, it is one of the simplest ways of providing additional, vicarious learning for participants.

Lecturettes are purposely simple and direct, with an emphasis on clarity and ease of presentation. They are not intended to be comprehensive or technical statements of theoretical positions. Each facilitator needs to develop a repertoire of theory and background that he can use in a variety of situations and activities.

One of Four Major Components

However valid the use of the lecturette may be, it is only one of four major components utilized in designing human relations laboratories.

The use of intensive small groups is the basic component of laboratory education. An almost endless variety of small groups exists, including the most common, the T-group (training group), the D-group (developmental group), or the N-group (new group).

Structured experiences of several types (e.g., ice breakers, dyadic designs, or communication activities) help to generate and focus the data of a laboratory. The facilitator will find that a given structured experience can be equally appropriate in a personal growth design or in a leadership development laboratory, depending on the way the data are processed.

Measurement devices—instruments—are another component of a human relations laboratory. They are useful in providing theory-based data with which participants can work in evaluating and understanding their learning experience.

Advantages of the Lecturette

The lecturette, as the fourth major component included in a human relations design can be used in several ways and for several purposes.

It can be delivered in large group sessions, commonly called "community" sessions. It can be used spontaneously in an intensive small-group session. It can be offered to participants as an introduction to a group activity, as handout material during the activity, or in a summary session.

When a lecturette is provided by the facilitator as a "cognitive map" for the experience that is to follow, it can be a guide for the participant in transferring his learning to his everyday experiences. As a method of focusing a participant's experiences in previous activities toward a theoretical model, it is highly effective. Thus the lecturette, when properly used, becomes a direct and useful means—for both participant and facilitator—of infusing cognitive material into the laboratory experience.

There is, of course, a potential pitfall in the use of lecturette material. We do not advocate "killing gnats with sledge hammers"; too much emphasis on cognitive material reduces its effectiveness. The lecturette, like many other tools, requires a deft touch.

A GUIDE TO PRESENTING LECTURETTES

The facilitator who wants to present effective, well-received lecturettes may find some of the following points helpful.

Taking Risks

Before the presentation, the facilitator needs to understand and consider his own motivations, his purposes for the lecturette, and his audience. Risk taking is, however, a necessary element in presenting effective lecturettes; the facilitator should allow for juggling alternatives, changing his mind, or offering unplanned asides. He can thus model risk-taking behavior for the participants.

A Positive Approach

It is important to start the lecturette with a positive approach. The facilitator should establish contact with his audience and prepare the participants by telling them what he is going to do and why he thinks it will be interesting to them.

Useful Aids

The general considerations to be taken into account in the facilitator's actual discourse are useful aids, content, and manner of presentation. Uncomplicated visual aids such as charts and graphs are a helpful device; so are concrete, specific, personalized examples with which the audience can identify.

Effectiveness of Content

Whatever the subject matter, the facilitator can increase its acceptability by reminding the participants why it is important. He can also use humor (best if pointed toward himself) to temper the intensity of the event. He can strive to avoid jargon. He can offer his own point of view about the material rather than simply report the ideas of others.

Presentation

How the facilitator presents the discourse is significant to its impact. Pacing the lecturette to accord with the audience is important. The facilitator should look for signs of puzzlement, incomprehension, or boredom, and he should slow down or speed up his presentation on the basis of these cues. Interrupting the discourse from time to time by initiating brief activities or by soliciting comments and examples from the audience also varies the pace of the presentation.

Voice modulation helps to keep the attention and interest of the audience; so does eye contact. The facilitator should also be aware of the physical setting in which he is operating and the body language he is using. Leftover posters tacked to the wall behind a speaker, for example, may present a continued, inappropriate distraction. Nervous or excessive gesturing may reduce the impact of what the facilitator is saying.

Except for direct quotations, the facilitator should not *read* his lecturette. Reading both reduces the personal touch and increases the audience's tendency to lose interest.

Since the presentation is oral, clarity is essential. A simple organization, a clearly delineated progression from point to point, appropriate restatements or recapitulations—these devices are simple but very helpful. It is often useful to present visually the outline of the lecturette.

Approach

Finally, the facilitator will be most effective if he is excited about his subject, enthusiastic, and natural and human in his reactions—clearly having fun himself. He should not be apologetic about the material or discount the value of what he is offering, but neither should he preach or berate opposing views.

When the facilitator has finished his presentation, he should summarize clearly, restating the significant points he has made; he should challenge his listeners to experiment with new behavior or new approaches; and he should encourage participants to take risks in applying new ideas.

Appropriately used and presented, the lecturette becomes an essential element—useful for both facilitator and participant—in a laboratory design or a workshop experience.

CLASSIFICATION OF LECTURETTES

Each of the eighty-nine lecturettes presented in the *Annuals* is categorized according to its primary emphasis. As is the case in each of the sections of the *Reference Guide to Handbooks and Annuals*, this classification is somewhat arbitrary. Categories established for this section are the following:

> Organizations
> Personal Growth
> Facilitation
> Communication
> Management/Leadership.

ORGANIZATIONS

Title	Author(s)	Volume & Page No.
Job Enrichment	F.V. Jessey	'72-127
Management by Objectives	T.M. Thomson	'72-130
An Introduction to PERT . . . Or . . .	D.E. Yoes	'72-135
Kurt Lewin's "Force Field Analysis"	M.S. Spier	'73-111
Three Approaches to Organizational Learning	A.J. Reilly	'73-130
Personal and Organizational Pain: Costs and Profits	P.J. Runkel	'74-148
Participatory Management: A New Morality	J.A. Stepsis	'75-120
Skill Climate and Organizational Blockages	D.L. Francis	'75-126
Open Systems	D.J. Marion	'75-132
Handling Group and Organizational Conflict	D.T. Simpson	'77-120
Organizational Norms	M. Alexander	'77-123
The Organizational Gestalt	P. Scholtes	'78-149
The Emotional Cycle of Change	D. Kelley & D.R. Conner	'79-117
The Systems View of Organizations: Dynamics of Organizational Change	P.R. Luciano	'79-140
Team Building from a Gestalt Perspective	H.B. Karp	'80-157
Dealing with Organizational Crises	M. Sashkin & J.E. Jones	'80-166
Coping with Anarchy in Organizations	M.A. Berger	'81-135

PERSONAL GROWTH

Title	Author(s)	Volume & Page No.
Risk-Taking and Error Protection Styles	J.E. Jones	'72-113
Defense Mechanisms in Groups	P. Thoresen	'72-117
Assumptions About the Nature of Man	J.E. Jones	'72-119
The Maslow Need Hierarchy	S.L. Pfeiffer	'72-125
The Johari Window: A Model for Soliciting and Giving Feedback	P.G. Hanson	'73-114
Risk-Taking	J.W. Pfeiffer	'73-124
Dependency and Intimacy	J.E. Jones	'73-132
Thinking and Feeling	A.G. Banet, Jr.	'73-139
Figure/Ground	J.A. Pfeiffer	'74-131
Humanistic Numbers	J.E. Jones	'75-115
Human Needs and Behavior	A.J. Reilly	'75-123
Re-Entry	J.E. Jones	'75-129
Assertion Theory	C. Kelley	'76-115
Interpersonal Feedback as Consensual Validation of Constructs	D.A. Devine	'76-124
Making Judgments Descriptive	A.C. Filley & L.A. Pace	'76-128
Power	D.C. King & J.C. Glidewell	'76-139
Centering	A.G. Banet, Jr.	'77-99
Androgyny	J. Campbell	'77-102
The Pendulum Swing: A Necessary Evil in the Growth Cycle	B.A. Gaw	'78-143
How to Maintain Personal Energy	J.E. Jones	'79-113
Jealousy: A Proactive Approach	C. Kelley	'80-138
Job-Related Adaptive Skills: Toward Personal Growth	J.J. Scherer	'80-152
Thinking About Feelings	W.C. Boshear	'81-117
Stress-Management Skills: Self-Modification for Personal Adjustment to Stress	L.P.K. LeGras	'81-138
Intrapersonal Conflict Resolution	H. Pates	'81-141

FACILITATION

Title	Author(s)	Volume & Page No.
Guidelines for Group Member Behavior	J.W. Pfeiffer	'72-109
A Model of Group Development	J.E. Jones	'73-127
Cog's Ladder: A Model of Group Development	G.O. Charrier	'74-142
Common Problems in Volunteer Groups	E. Bancroft	'75-111
Wishes and Fears	A.G. Banet, Jr.	'75-118
Training Components for Group Facilitators	R.K. Conyne	'75-138
Therapy or Personal Growth?	T.A. Boone	'75-141
Alternatives to Theorizing	S.M. Herman	'76-143
Strategies for Designing an Intervention	G.H. Varney	'78-133
Contracting: A Process and a Tool	F.L. Ulschak	'78-138

COMMUNICATION

Title	Author(s)	Volume & Page No.
Synergy and Consensus-Seeking	J.E. Jones	'73-108
Conditions Which Hinder Effective Communication	J.W. Pfeiffer	'73-120
Confrontation: Types, Conditions, and Outcomes	R.R. Kurtz & J.E. Jones	'73-135
Five Components Contributing to Effective Interpersonal Communications	M.R. Chartier	'74-125
Making Requests Through Metacommunication	C.M. Rossiter, Jr.	'74-129
The Interpersonal Contract	C.G. Carney & S.L. McMahon	'74-135
Communication Patterns in Organization Structure	D.L. Ford, Jr., & O. Elliott	'74-150
Dealing with Anger	J.E. Jones & A.G. Banet, Jr.	'76-111
The Awareness Wheel	S. Miller, E.W. Nunnally, & D.B. Wackman	'76-120
D-I-D: A Three-Dimensional Model for Understanding Group Communication	D.G. Smith	'77-106

COMMUNICATION (Continued)

Title	Author(s)	Volume & Page No.
Constructive Conflict in Discussions: Learning to Management Disagreements Effectively	J.T. Wood	'77-115
Communication Effectiveness: Active Listening and Sending Feeling Messages	J.N. Wismer	'78-119
Communicating Communication	J.R. Luthi	'78-123
Anybody with Eyes Can See the Facts!	A. Kuperman	'79-128
The Four-Communication-Styles Approach	T. Carney	'80-127
Interaction Process Analysis	B. Byrum-Gaw	'80-133
Defensive and Supportive Communication	G.W. Combs	'81-113
Kenepathy	M. Stimac	'81-124

MANAGEMENT/LEADERSHIP

Title	Author(s)	Volume & Page No.
McGregor's Theory X-Theory Y Model	A.J. Robinson	'72-121
Criteria of Effective Goal-Setting: The SPIRO Model	J.E. Jones	'72-133
Win/Lose Situations	G.E. Wiley	'73-105
Hidden Agendas		'74-133
Conflict-Resolution Strategies	J.A. Stepsis	'74-139
The "Shouldist" Manager	S.M. Herman	'74-146
The Supervisor as Counselor	R.A. Zawacki & P.E. LaSota	'75-135
Leadership as Persuasion and Adaptation	J.T. Wood	'76-132
Role Functions in a Group	D. Nylen, J.R. Mitchell, & A. Stout	'76-136
A Practical Leadership Paradigm	T.A. Boone	'77-110
Tolerance of Equivocality: The Bronco, Easy Rider, Blockbuster, and Nomad	R.C. Rodgers	'78-128
Encouraging Others to Change Their Behavior	J.C. Morton & D.M. Blair	'79-123

MANAGEMENT/LEADERSHIP (Continued)

Title	Author(s)	Volume & Page No.
The Centered Boss	P. Scholtes	'79-133
Transactions in the Change Process	T.R. Harvey	'79-136
Dimensions of Role Efficacy	U. Pareek	'80-143
A Nine-Step Problem-Solving Model	L.C. Earley & P.B. Rutledge	'80-146
Dealing with Disruptive Individuals in Meetings	J.E. Jones	'80-161
Creativity and Creative Problem Solving	M.B. Ross	'81-129

INTRODUCTION TO THEORY AND PRACTICE PAPERS

In leadership and management development, in organization development, in the consulting process, in the whole human relations training field, we believe that the most critical component is the personal, *human* element. Theory, technique, and research are important and invaluable, but they should be seen in perspective, against a framework of the human, the personal, the individual, the practical, the *real*.

DIMENSIONS OF FACILITATOR EFFECTIVENESS

The Person
Empathy
Acceptance

Congruence
Flexibility

Skills
Listening
Expressing Oneself
Observing

Responding
Intervening
Designing

Techniques
Structured Experiences
Instruments
Lecturettes

Confrontations
Interventions (Verbal and Nonverbal)

Theories
Personality
Group Dynamics
Organizational Behavior

Systems
Community Behavior

The Person

Social ills continue to plague us despite our current, incredible, brilliant technology. We need to learn more about our own interpersonal relationships—and this is what human relations training is about. The common denominator is the *person*. To become better as a facilitator, one must become better as a person.

One of the significant personal dimensions is the ability to *feel empathy* for another person. Complete empathy is not possible, of course; we can never experience someone else's situation exactly as he does. But we can try to see things from another person's perspective; this effort is critical.

Acceptance is another important personal dimension-allowing another person to be different, to have a different set of values and goals, to behave differently. Rogers calls this Unconditional Positive Regard (UPR).

Congruence and *flexibility* determine two additional aspects of the person. A congruent person is aware of himself and what he is feeling and is able to communicate that self to another person in a straightforward way. He is healthy and psychologically mature. A flexible person is not dogmatic, opinionated, rigid, or authoritarian. As a consultant, he should be able to deal with another person at that person's pace.

If people have these personal attributes, they are therapeutic. Just being around them makes others feel good; they help by being well-integrated persons themselves.

The most meaningful direction a consultant can take is toward improving his own personal development, furthering his own understanding of his values, attitudes, impulses, and desires. Two major interpersonal conflicts that a facilitator must be able to resolve for himself are his capacity for intimacy and his relation to authority.

Important as the personal dimension is, however, there are other components involved in successful human relations training.

Skills

Certain basic communication skills are necessary in order to promote individual, group, and organizational growth. A facilitator needs to develop his ability to *listen*, to *express* himself (both verbally and nonverbally), to *observe*, to *respond* to people, to *intervene* artfully in the group process, and to *design* effective learning environments that make efficient use of resources.

Techniques

One can also heighten and improve the effect of human relations training through certain techniques. Structured experiences, instruments, lecturettes, confrontations, and verbal and nonverbal interventions are all useful in increasing a facilitator's effectiveness.

Theories

Theory is a resource. It is one of the components a facilitator uses to develop and improve himself as a practitioner.

Theories abound in the human relations field; there are theories of personality, group dynamics, organizational behavior, community behavior, and systems. Systems theory, for example, has some interesting implications for OD in that it points out that all systems are interdependent and no one can be dealt with in isolation.

Practice

At the moment, human relations practitioners are far ahead of theorists: the tendency is to try out an idea and see if it works first and then to find the research underpinnings necessary for its justification. Explanation follows practice.

Theory and research are inextricably intertwined with practice—one requires the other. Yet if the choice had to be made between a brilliant theorist, thoroughly grounded in technique and theory, and a stimulating, effective consultant with a well-integrated personal self—our choice would be the latter.

PERSPECTIVE ON HUMAN RELATIONS TRAINING

Four streams of work characterize the field of human relations training at this time. Quite a number of group facilitators focus their attention on the area of personal growth, numerous people are concerned primarily with leadership and management development, growing numbers of consultants are working in organization development, and a smaller but significant minority is involved in community development. The major element that exists across these spheres of interest is the use of intensive small groups as interventions in training activities.

The accompanying chart illustrates some of the overlap and the interests among the four major areas of activity within the field of human relations training.

The Four Major Areas of Activity in Human Relations Training

	Individual	Group	Organization	Community
I N T R A	**Personal Growth** sensory awareness value clarification life planning	**Personal Growth** **Leadership Development** **Organization Development** group dynamics team building	**Organization Development** systems climate assessment problem solving	**Community Development**
I N T E R	**Personal Growth** **Leadership Development** communication skills human interaction management development	**Leadership Development** **Organization Development** negotiation skills group dynamics	**Organization Development** **Community Development** mergers	

The four columns of the chart are cumulative to the right; that is, the *individual* is the basic ingredient of the *group*, which is the basic building block of *organizations*, which make up the basis of *communities*. Within each of these four classifications there is an *intra* and *inter* dimension. The *intra-individual* cell of the chart represents the locus of personal growth activities. We are concerned in personal growth with helping individual participants grow in awareness of their feelings, attitudes, values, and self-concepts, and these traits are presumed to be primarily intraphysic.

In the *interindividual* cell of the chart we see that personal growth activities and leadership development activities overlap in their emphasis on human interaction. Both leadership and management development, on the one hand, and personal growth activities, on the other, share a common concern with building skills for effective human relations, such as listening, expressing oneself, and responding to others.

In the *intragroup* cell of the chart, we can see that facilitators have as a common basis an emphasis on understanding and intervening in group dynamics. Intragroup phenomena such as participation, influence, decision making, task vs. process orientation, etc., become the basis for many interventions in personal growth, leadership development, and organization development. Organizations are primarily made up of individual people who are members of overlapping, embedded groups, and the consultant needs to be sensitive to the fact that the dynamics within the groups can materially affect the problem-solving capability of the organization. Team building has a great deal in common with both leadership development and personal growth training. It is little wonder, then, that group facilitators most often enter organization development at the level of team building.

Leadership development and organization development workers share a common interest in studying *intergroup* phenomena. Such aspects of organizational life as cooperation and competition across groups, sharing of information, etc., become a concern both in training leaders and in working real organizational issues.

The core of organization development is in the *intraorganization* cell of the chart. The OD consultant is concerned with monitoring and intervening in such systemic processes as influence, communication patterns, morale, and utilization of human resources. The effort is to look at the total organization as composed of interdependent subsystems.

It is in the *interorganization* sphere that OD specialists and community development workers share a common interest. Communities can be seen as comprised of relatively autonomous but interdependent organizations. These may be schools, churches, manufacturing organizations, businesses, etc., which may or may not recognize their dependency on each other. The OD consultant is concerned with seeing how the organization "interfaces" with its environment, including its customers and suppliers and pressure groups in the environment, such as the government and political organizations. The community development consultant is concerned with how the organizations in a given community interrelate in ways that affect the "common good."

There are basically two types of community-development change agents. The activists, trained in political power interventions and characterized by Saul Alinsky and

Cesar Chavez, advocate particular types of community reform through the use of collective strategies for garnering power. The applied-behavioral-science-oriented consultant, however, operates primarily from a confrontive stance, in which he attempts to get organizations in the community to look at the processes through which they relate to each other, in order to increase their ability to collaborate. His job is the most complex in the four types of human relations training activities, in that he has to deal with highly mixed motives, and often he has to rely on volunteers to carry out decisions spawned by the processes he has sponsored.

The complexity in human relations training has accumulated with its emergent technology. The emphasis on personal development has been traditional almost from the beginning of the development of this field. Organization development has a relatively brief history compared with management development, and community development as an applied behavioral science field is largely embryonic.

CLASSIFICATION OF THEORY AND PRACTICE PAPERS

The eighty-seven papers published in the Theory and Practice sections of the *Annuals* fall into six categories:

> Organization Development
> Design
> Communication
> Models
> Facilitation
> Research.

We have not attempted to maintain a balanced distribution of articles in these categories in the papers we publish. The *Annual* serves a function quite different from scholarly journals; its materials are written and edited to be immediately useful to the practitioner.

ORGANIZATION DEVELOPMENT

Title	Author(s)	Volume & Page No.
An Introduction to Organization Development	J.J. Sherwood	'72-153
Seven Pure Strategies of Change	K.E. Olmosk	'72-163
Notes on Freedom	S.M. Herman	'72-211
Planned Renegotiation: A Norm-Setting OD Intervention	J.J. Sherwood & J.C. Glidewell	'73-195
Some Implications of Value Clarification for Organization Development	M. Smith	'73-203
The Sensing Interview	J.E. Jones	'73-213
An Informal Glossary of Terms and Phrases in Organization Development	P.B. Vaill	'73-235
Individual Needs and Organizational Goals: An Experiential Lecture	A.J. Reilly	'74-215
Basic Concepts of Survey Feedback	D.G. Bowers & J.L. Franklin	'74-221

ORGANIZATION DEVELOPMENT (Continued)

Title	Author(s)	Volume & Page No.
Team-Building	A.J. Reilly & J.E. Jones	'74-227
The Shadow of Organization Development	S.M. Herman	'74-239
Managing the Dynamics of Change and Stability	A. Broskowski, W.L. Mermis, Jr., & F. Khajavi	'75-173
The White Paper: A Tool for OD	T.H. Patten, Jr.	'75-195
Understanding Your Organization's Character	R. Harrison	'75-199
A Gestalt Approach to Collaboration in Organizations	H.B. Karp	'76-203
A Current Assessment of OD: What It Is and Why It Often Fails	J.W. Pfeiffer & J.E. Jones	'76-225
Team Development: A Training Approach	L.N. Solomon	'77-181
Intervening in Organizations Through Reward Systems	T.H. Patten, Jr.	'77-195
Constructive Citizen Participation	D.M. Connor	'77-209
Utilizing Human Resources: Individual Versus Group Approaches to Problem Solving and Decision Making	J.J. Sherwood & F.J. Hoylman	'78-157
Types of Process Interventions	A.M. Freedman	'78-163
OD Readiness	J.W. Pfeiffer & J.E. Jones	'78-219
The Behavioral Science Roots of Organization Development: An Integrated Perspective	T.H. Patten, Jr.	'79-194
Alternative Data-Feedback Designs for Organizational Intervention	D.A. Nadler	'79-221
Consultation to Human-Service Programs	L.D. Goodstein	'80-213
Evaluation of Human-Service Programs	K.S. Trisko & V.C. League	'80-224
Multiple Measures to Assess the Impact of Organization Development Interventions	D.L. Lockwood & F. Luthans	'80-233
Developing Collaboration in Organizations	U. Pareek	'81-165

ORGANIZATION DEVELOPMENT (Continued)

Title	Author(s)	Volume & Page No.
Human Resource Development: What It Is and How to Become Involved	J.E. Jones	'81-188
An Overview of Ten Management and Organizational Theorists	M. Sashkin	'81-206
A Method for Structured Naturalistic Observation of Organizational Behavior	D.N.T. Perkins, D.A. Nadler, & M.D. Hanlon	'81-222

DESIGN

Title	Author(s)	Volume & Page No.
Contracts in Encounter Groups	G. Egan	'72-185
The Concept of Structure in Experiential Learning	R.R. Middleman & G. Goldberg	'72-203
Counseling and Clinical Training Applications of Human Relations Theory and Practice	R. Levin	'72-225
Design Considerations in Laboratory Education	J.W. Pfeiffer & J.E. Jones	'73-177
A Two-Phase Approach to Human Relations Training	G. Egan	'73-225
Life/Work Planning	A.G. Kirn & M. Kirn	'74-189
Cybernetic Sessions: A Technique for Gathering Ideas	J.T. Hall & R.A. Dixon	'74-197
The Experiential Learning Model and Its Application to Large Groups	S.E. Marks & W.L. Davis	'75-161
Applied Group Problem-Solving: The Nominal Group Technique	D.L. Ford, Jr., & P.M. Nemiroff	'75-179
Designing and Facilitating Experiential Group Activities: Variables and Issues	C.L. Cooper & K. Harrison	'76-157
The Delphi Technique: A Projection Tool for Serious Inquiry	R.L. Bunning	'79-174
Meeting Management	D. Nicoll	'81-183

COMMUNICATION

Title	Author(s)	Volume & Page No.
Communication Modes: An Experiential Lecture	J.E. Jones	'72-173
Openness, Collusion and Feedback	J.W. Pfeiffer & J.E. Jones	'72-197
"Don't You Think That...?": An Experiential Lecture on Indirect and Direct Communication	J.W. Pfeiffer & J.E. Jones	'74-203
Giving Feedback: An Interpersonal Skill	P.G. Hanson	'75-147
Nonverbal Communication and the Intercultural Encounter	M. Schnapper	'75-155
Clarity of Expression in Interpersonal Communication	M.R. Chartier	'76-149

MODELS

Title	Author(s)	Volume & Page No.
Types of Growth Groups	J.E. Jones	'72-145
TORI Theory and Practice	J.R. Gibb	'72-157
Transcendence Theory	J.W. Pfeiffer	'72-179
A Transactional Analysis Primer	J.P. Anderson	'73-145
Hill Interaction Matrix (HIM) Conceptual Framework for Understanding Groups	W.F. Hill	'73-159
Models and Roles of Change Agents	M. Sashkin	'74-209
A Gestalt Primer	J.W. Pfeiffer & J.A. Pfeiffer	'75-183
Dimensions of the Organizational Universe: A Model for Assessment and Direction	D.J. Marion	'75-211

MODELS (Continued)

Title	Author(s)	Volume & Page No.
Yin/Yang: A Perspective on Theories of Group Development	A.G. Banet, Jr.	'76-169
Interrole Exploration	U. Pareek	'76-211
A Tavistock Primer	A.G. Banet, Jr., & C. Hayden	'77-155
Structure as an Integrative Concept in Management Theory and Practice	J.A. Stepsis	'77-169
Personal Effectiveness	U. Pareek	'78-170
Loevinger's Ego States as the Basis of an Intervention Model	V. Pinedo, Jr.	'78-192
Behavioral Clarity in Consultation: The Triadic Model as Instrument	G. Egan	'78-204
Finishing Unfinished Business: Creative Problem Solving	F.L. Ulschak	'79-154
A Practical Model of Motivation and Character Development	R. Harrison	'79-207
Methods of Centering	A.G. Banet, Jr.	'80-175
Learning Cycles: Models of Behavioral Change	A.B. Palmer	'81-147
The Organizational Universe	J.E. Jones	'81-155
An Adlerian Primer	D.G. Eckstein	'81-193

FACILITATION

Title	Author(s)	Volume & Page No.
Therapeutic Intervention and the Perception of Process	A.G. Banet, Jr.	'74-179
Co-Facilitating	J.W. Pfeiffer & J.E. Jones	'75-219
Working with Couples: Some Basic Considerations	H.A. Otto	'76-185
Fantasy: Theory and Technique	A.G. Banet, Jr., & J.E. Jones	'76-191

FACILITATION (Continued)

RESEARCH

INTRODUCTION TO AND CLASSIFICATION OF RESOURCES

In recent years there has been a phenomenal growth in the human relations training field. The availability of materials and services has increased to the point that it is difficult to maintain a current understanding of resources available to the group facilitator and OD consultant.

The classification of the material in the Resources sections of the *Annuals* is as follows:

> Bibliography
> Professional Affiliations
> International
> Personal Growth Approaches
> Product Sources

Readers who are familiar with previous editions of the *Reference Guide* will note that the "Book Reviews" classification has been eliminated in this edition. The last book review to appear in an *Annual* was in 1977; since that time the book-review function has been assumed by another of our publications, *Group & Organization Studies: The International Journal for Group Facilitators*. This creates room for additional resources in the *Annual*. Large-scale, topical book reviews from previous *Annuals* are now listed under the "Bibliography" classification since they are, in effect, annotated bibliographies of books in a particular subject area.

BIBLIOGRAPHY

Title	Author(s)	Volume & Page No.
A Step Toward Definition: Review of *The Addison-Wesley Series on Organization Development*	T. Lyons	'72-266
A Personalized Human Relations Training Bibliography	M. Smith	'73-247
A Bibliography of Small-Group Training, 1973-1974	W.B. Reddy	'75-264
A Reference List for Change Agents	L.E. Pate	'76-241
Humanistic Education: A Review of Books Since 1970	P.A. Schmuck & R.A. Schmuck	'76-265

BIBLIOGRAPHY (Continued)

Title	Author(s)	Volume & Page No.
Values Clarification: A Review of Major Books	J. Goodman	'76-274
Transactional Analysis: A Review of the Literature	H. Capers	'76-280
A Bibliography of Nonverbal Communication	R.W. Rasberry	'77-227
A Bibliography of Small-Group Training, 1974-1976	W.B. Reddy & K. Lippert	'77-238
Assertion: The Literature Since 1970	C. Kelley	'77-264
Organization Development: A Review of Recent Books (1973-1976)	M. Sashkin	'77-276
Humanistic and Transpersonal Education: A Guide to Resources	J. Canfield	'78-277
Small-Group Behavior and Development: A Selective Bibliography	G. Hearn	'79-252
A Brief Glossary of Frequently Used Terms in Organization Development and Planned Change	M. Sashkin	'80-249
Career Development: Literature and Resources	H.L. Fromkin & J.D. McDonald	'80-285
Periodicals in Organization Development and Related Fields	S.M. Rosenthal & L.P. Church	'81-259
Annotated Bibliography on Power in Organizations	M. Smith & H.L. Fromkin	'81-269
A Bibliography of Small-Group Training, 1976-1979	W.B. Reddy & K.M. Lippert	'81-284

PROFESSIONAL AFFILIATIONS

Title	Author(s)	Volume & Page No.
The International Association of Applied Social Scientists	K.D. Benne & S.J. Ruma	'72-141
Alphabet Soup	F. Johnson	'72-231
Growth Centers	W. Swartley	'73-267

PROFESSIONAL AFFILIATIONS (Continued)

Title	Author(s)	Volume & Page No.
AHP Growth Center List	Association for Humanistic Psychology	'74-255
Applied Behavioral Science Consulting Organizations: A Directory		'75-249
AHP Growth Center List	Association for Humanistic Psychology	'77-252
Graduate Programs in Applied Behavioral Science: A Directory	S. Campbell	'78-229
AHP Growth Center List, 1978		'79-270
Alphabet Soup: 1980	F.P. Johnson	'80-265
Applied Behavioral Science Consulting Organizations: An Updated Directory		'80-271

INTERNATIONAL

Title	Author(s)	Volume & Page No.
Human Relations Training in the UK and Continental Europe	C.L. Cooper	'74-249
Canada's Experience with Human Relations Training	H.G. Dimock	'75-233

PERSONAL GROWTH APPROACHES

Title	Author(s)	Volume & Page No.
Awareness Through Movement	M. Feldenkrais	'75-238
An Introduction to Structural Integration (Rolfing)	R. Pierce	'75-241
What is Psychosynthesis?		'75-246
Bioenergetic Therapy	P. Katz	'76-235
Hatha Yoga	L.C. Trueblood	'76-238

PRODUCT SOURCES

Title	Author(s)	Volume & Page No.
Games and Simulations: Materials, Sources, and Learning Concepts	B.D. Ruben	'72-235
Media Resources for Human Relations Training	N. Felsenthal	'72-241
Selecting Workshop Sites	T.A. Boone & R.A. Reid	'78-253
Human Relations Films for Group Facilitators	D.L. Smith	'78-260
Using a Video System in Human Relations Training Video Feedback in Groups and Organizations	D. Francis	'79-239
Selecting an Appropriate Video System	A.R. Davidson	'79-245
Facilitating Simulation Games	M.R. Chartier	'81-247

NAME INDEX

TITLE INDEX